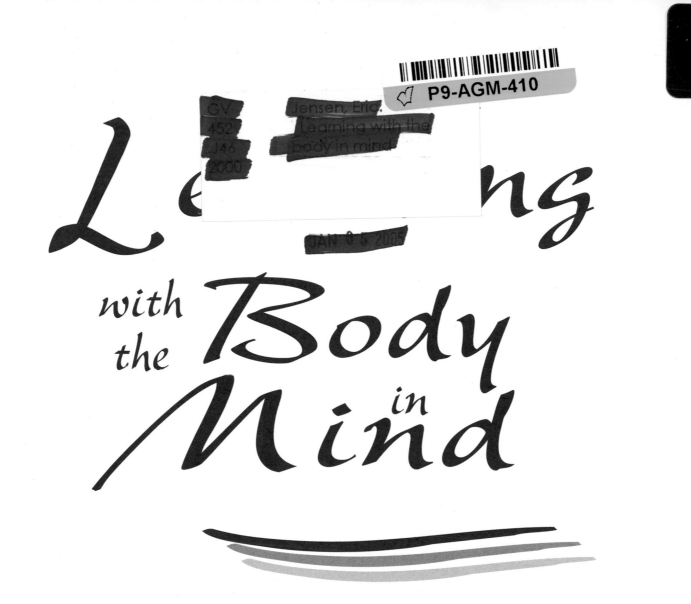

Learning

with the Body in Mind

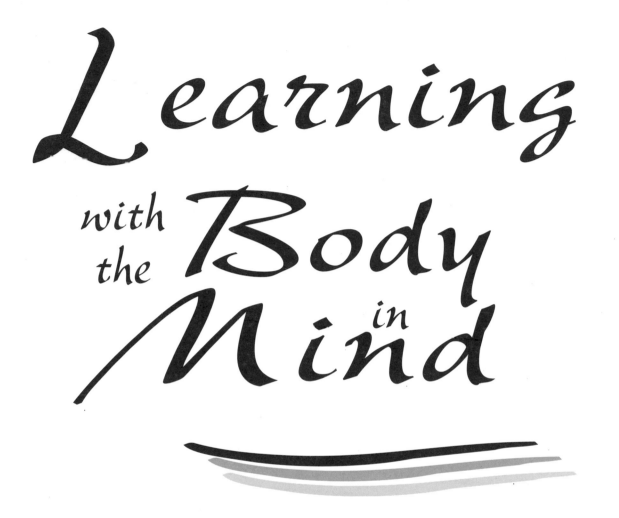

Learning with the Body in Mind

The Scientific Basis for Energizers, Movement, Play, Games, and Physical Education

Eric Jensen

Learning with the Body in Mind:

The Scientific Basis for Energizers, Movement, Play, Games, and Physical Education

©2000 The Brain Store®, Inc.
Layout and Design: Tracy Linares
Editing: Karen Markowitz

Acknowledgments:
Heartfelt thanks to the many "activity advocates," who over the years have supported the value of movement in education in spite of the scientific and administrative hurdles and unknowns. We've entered a new era in which not only our hearts and bodies recognize the value of active learning, but science too has stood up and taken notice. Here's to the pioneers in movement education and to the science that now supports our work. Special thanks also to Dr. Rich Allen for his game and energizer suggestions... Cheers!

Printed in the United States of America
Published by The Brain Store®, Inc.
San Diego, CA, USA

ISBN #1-890460-07-9

For additional copies or bulk discounts contact:

The Brain Store®, Inc.
4202 Sorrento Valley Blvd., #B
San Diego, CA 92121
Phone (858) 546-7555 • Fax (858) 546-7560
E-mail: info@thebrainstore.com
Web site: www.thebrainstore.com

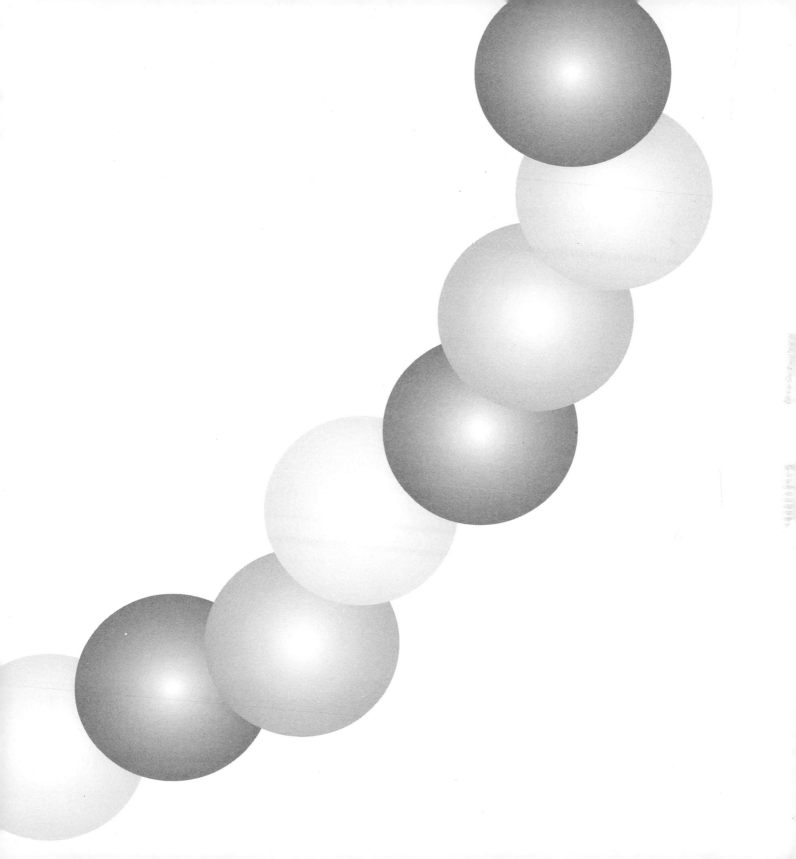

Table of Contents

Introduction

The primary objective of this book is to create a context for active learning—that is, where movement, play, and exercise belong in relation to what and how we learn. I am not an athlete, nor am I a frustrated ex-athlete trying to further a personal cause. I have never participated in theater arts, nor do I possess anything other than marginal dance skills. While I occasionally play a sport (I like to surf, golf, and work out), I'm not really very good at any of them. And yet, I've learned that when my body is engaged, my mind is engaged. Whether I'm great at the activity or terrible, it doesn't matter. What matters is the dynamics involved: When we move, we groove. My own experiences in school, probably much like yours, paint a classic picture of movement activities relegated to recess or P.E. class. Otherwise, we were expected to sit in our seats in subordinated posture for endless desensitizing hours.

Ask a hundred adults what their overall impression of school was and most will say "monotony." While I fall into this category, as well, I do remember enjoying every opportunity to move, play sports, or just do things. What I dreaded was the daily numbing despair of sitting and passively listening. Now that science supports what some savvy educators have known intuitively all along—that movement enhances learning—it is time to integrate this knowledge into our lesson plans. This book is a companion for that process.

I hope that *Learning with the Body in Mind* inspires educators to think about movement activities in a whole new way. It's easy to say that some of our learners are more kinesthetic, so therefore we ought to add more activity, but it's an entirely different matter to understand the very nature of learning itself and to bring the science of learning into our educational contexts. While there's a great deal of research going on, there is also a virtual mountain of data that is being ignored—data that clearly support the importance of movement at every age, from toddlerhood through adulthood.

Finally, I'd like us to think about some of the challenges we face in schools and consider the possibility that the solution has been under our noses all along. Many of our classroom problems will decline as learners become engaged. From improved social skills through game interaction to motivation of the "hard-to-reach" through outward bound or challenge courses, energizers, team play, and other movement challenges, the field is wide open. We know that apathy in the classroom improves as sensory activation and hands-on learning are increased. As learning institutions incorporate more physical activity and less lecture, all of our students, not just the kinesthetic learners or those lacking social skills, will experience increased intrinsic motivation, improved attitudes, more bonding, and yes, even more brain cells. In fact, when it comes down to it, most of our problems can be solved through purposeful integration of active learning. When this is the mind-set of every educator, not just physical education teachers, we will see a dramatic reduction in student behavior issues and learning problems.

Ultimately, this book is about getting positive results with all learners. It's about re-educating our largely activity-phobic education system so that we reach a far greater percentage of students. The scope of movement activities here includes recess, dance, play, theater, games, energizers, and physical education. Are you ready to explore the possibility that more activity, more wisely applied, will make a significant, positive, and lasting contribution to today's learners? Are you ready for some modern day miracles? If so, let's get moving!

A Note About the Research

Although my approach to this book puts the human brain up front and center, the integrated human ecosystem that encompasses mind-and-body in all endeavors is really at the heart of my work. As much as possible (without overdoing the scientific or technical), I used data from anatomy, physiology, and neuroscience to help form a hypothesis about why the movement strategies presented in this book might work. To support the hypothesis, I looked for clinical and educational trials that were peer-reviewed and employed valid research designs. Every effort was made to select from reliable sources with supporting data.

But even with strong supporting data, you and I know that some educators will still ignore the findings. Some teachers will maintain that it's up to students themselves to be motivated, alert, and interested. But I argue differently. I believe times have changed. Teachers who depend on content as their only asset are dinosaurs. Today's learners have masses of information at their fingertips. The point is, the role of today's educator is not to provide content, but to engage learners with relevant content in meaningful ways so that it is learned, valued, and hopefully, enjoyed—not just "covered." Because movement engages the brain as well as the body, it is the wise educator's trump card.

The larger point here is that we all (I trust) share the same mission. We all want to make a positive, significant contribution to our learners' lives. And since each student is unique, our methodology must reflect many diverse shapes, sizes, formats, and packages to successfully appeal to every learner. So far, there's no "magic bullet" for learning. Movement-based learning is not a panacea to solve all of education's problems, and anyone who represents such a perspective is misleading others. There are many ways to learn, and active learning is just one of them. It's a good one, but it's just one of them.

Nevertheless, nothing is more relevant to learning than our brain, and ultimately, the integration of our mind-body system into the learning environment. The future belongs to those with vision who can grasp not only the trends, but the importance of them. This is not to say, however, that changing classroom practice will be easy. The long-standing habit of having students sit passively while the "Big Cheese" stands and delivers can be a hard habit to break. The integration of brain research into our everyday lives is happening all around us, but it will take time and a concerted effort. The time, however, to jump on the bandwagon is now! *Let's move on!*

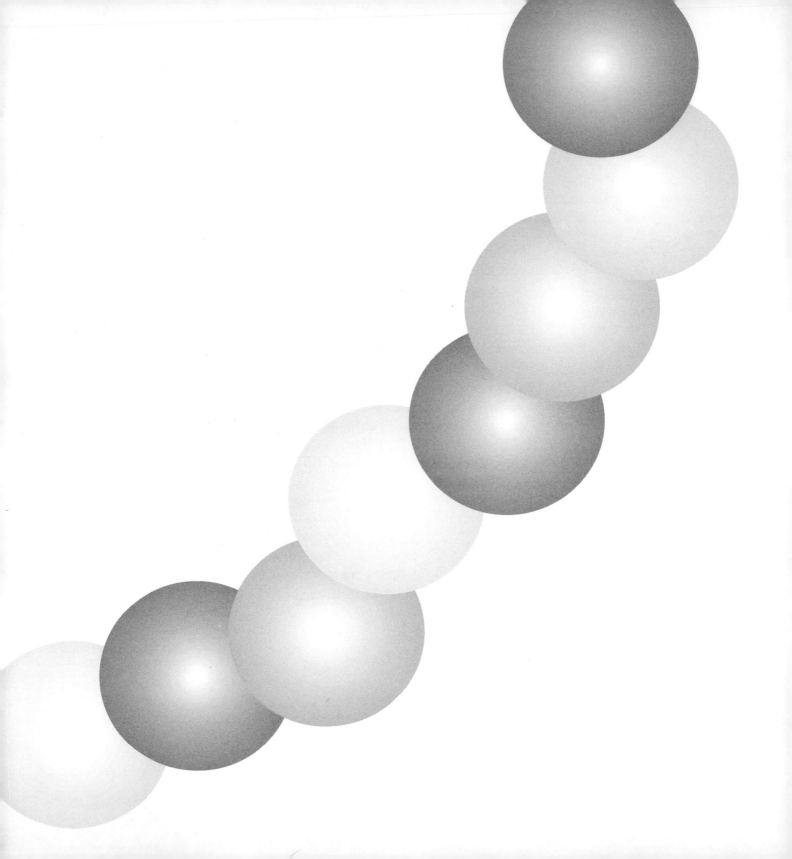

After all the arguments have been
made for one side or the other,
it gets down to one thing:
Movement is about living
and living is about learning.

—Eric Jensen

CHAPTER ONE

The Nature of Implicit Learning

There's a way of thinking about learning that might change how you view the power of movement activities. Dance, theater, physical education, recess, aerobics, energizers, sports, and simple games all elicit a different kind of learning: one that is centered in the body. We call this kind of learning *implicit*. While the more common, test-oriented, *explicit* learning (lecture, textbooks, research, video, and discussion) is more overt and labeled, implicit learning happens without labels.

Implicit learning is the acquisition of knowledge that takes place primarily outside of our conscious awareness. Although, there are various ways that implicit knowledge is acquired, we don't usually recognize or label the learning at the time it is happening. Movement provides just one vehicle for eliciting implicit learning, but it is a very powerful one. Other experiences that seem to encode implicit learning include trauma (emotional learning), stimulus-response (the hot stove effect), synthesis (whereby patterns are extracted from raw information), procedural learning (like riding a bike), and imitation (whereby learning is encoded through observation).

To Understand It Is to Love It

Think about it this way: If you didn't change a light bulb for five years, would you still know how to do it? Or, if you learned the names of the world's five largest rivers, but hadn't thought about them in five years, would you still be able to list them? The likely answer is yes to the light bulb and no to the river question. Why? Because the first question represents implicit knowledge, while the second represents explicit knowledge. Your body remembers how to change a light bulb, even if your brain has forgotten the names of the largest rivers.

Cognitive scientists break down learning in various ways; however, implicit (also known as reflexive or procedural) and explicit (also known as semantic or episodic) are two of the most common distinctions. Researchers believe that these two systems operate somewhat independently, but have some overlap. This book will explore how and why implicit learning—learning by doing—may be far more important than you thought.

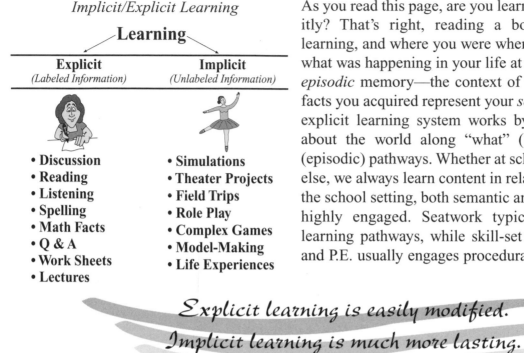

Implicit/Explicit Learning

Learning

Explicit *(Labeled Information)*	Implicit *(Unlabeled Information)*
• Discussion	• Simulations
• Reading	• Theater Projects
• Listening	• Field Trips
• Spelling	• Role Play
• Math Facts	• Complex Games
• Q & A	• Model-Making
• Work Sheets	• Life Experiences
• Lectures	

As you read this page, are you learning explicitly or implicitly? That's right, reading a book represents explicit learning, and where you were when you read this book and what was happening in your life at the time represents your *episodic* memory—the context of the learning—while the facts you acquired represent your *semantic* memory. So our explicit learning system works by gathering information about the world along "what" (semantic) and "where" (episodic) pathways. Whether at school, home, or anywhere else, we always learn content in relationship to a context. In the school setting, both semantic and episodic pathways are highly engaged. Seatwork typically engages semantic learning pathways, while skill-set learning typical of arts and P.E. usually engages procedural learning pathways.

Explicit learning is easily modified.
Implicit learning is much more lasting.

The implicit system, in contrast, works by organizing our responses to the world around us. These responses include the "knee-jerk" reactions and conditioned responses of reflexive learning and the more measured operational, skill-based, or "how to" responses of procedural learning. Implicit and explicit learning systems operate conjunctively. First we take in the information around us, then we organize our responses to it.

Before going any further, however, let me present an important caveat. While I've pointed out general differences between explicit (the more overt) and implicit (the more covert) types of learning, *there is really no clean distinction.* Learning that begins as explicit may become implicit

Implicit/Explicit Learning

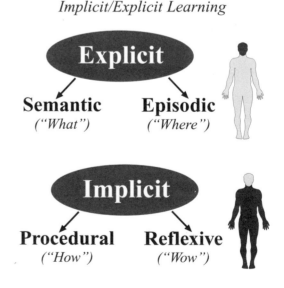

Explicit

Semantic → ← Episodic
("What") *("Where")*

Implicit

Procedural → ← Reflexive
("How") *("Wow")*

over time (i.e., reading about how to do a task, then doing the task, then forgetting what you read). Or, learning that begins as explicit (playing a sport), then becomes implicit (coaching the sport). It is helpful to think of the two systems as bicycle wheels that turn together to move you along. If one is flat, progress is stalled. I have "separated" the wheels here for instructive purposes only.

Ten Reasons for Increasing Implicit Learning

While I'm not suggesting that one wheel is better than the other, I am suggesting that both are just as important. Having said that, implicit learning is special for many reasons. It is, in fact, much more reliable than the traditional textbook-driven explicit approach to teaching and learning, and here's why:

Robustness	The effects are greater with more duration. A person can absorb more information per day through implicit channels. The length of time that implicit learning lasts is significantly longer than that of explicit learning. There's a large, unambiguous data base that supports the size and magnitude of in-the-body learning (Greenwald 1992).
Independent of Age	Newborn babies to senior citizens (and every age group between) demonstrate the ability to learn and retain implicit knowledge (Parkin and Streete 1988). It's limitless.
Ease of Learning	A great deal of implicit learning is transmitted via role-modeling, observation, trial and error, experimentation, and peer demonstrations (Reber 1993). Neurophysiologists are presently exploring the idea that the human brain forms very simple and predictable inputs that over time become massive and complex neural networks. These parallel systems have been computer modeled and applied to implicit learning with good success (Jennings and Keele 1991), suggesting that the connectionist model may be responsible for easy, yet ultimately complex learning. We also now have a better understanding of the cortical mechanisms for imitation, another form of implicit learning and one of the easiest of all learning types (Iacoboni, et al. 1999).

Cross-Cultural Transmission	With robust effects across a wide spectrum of human cultures and a low variability from one individual to the next, the argument for implicit learning is an easy one to make. From urban to rural, from state to state, and from country to country, is there really much difference in how people learn? In the hands-on real world of life, there are very few differences.
Independent of Intelligence	Implicit task learning reveals little concordance with typical, older-style measures of intelligence such as IQ tests (Reber, et al. 1991). However, Dr. Frank Wilson, author of *The Hand* (1998), discovered that individuals whose work involves extensive implicit knowledge and hand coordination, such as jugglers, neurosurgeons, puppeteers, and mountain climbers, exhibit similar IQ levels and learning capacity.
Efficiency	Because implicit learning takes place outside of a student's conscious awareness, it requires few attentional resources. One can, and often does, learn both explicitly and implicitly at the same time. Go for a bike ride with a friend and you'll acquire content information, learn rules about bicycling, draw generalized conclusions about your friend and yourself, while never thinking about learning these things.
Value	The more complex the skill set or content knowledge, the harder it is to explain it. Ask a ten-year-old how to hit a golf ball and you'll probably get a simple, straightforward answer like, "Just swing at it!" Ask Tiger Woods, however, the same question and the answer will probably be, "It has to 'feel right.'" Whether we're trying to master a sport or master the art of teaching, most problems are solved by "feel," which is ultimately implicit learning.

Integrity

Implicit learning is less susceptible to brain insults, Alzheimer's damage, dyslexia, aphasia, drug usage, and memory decay. Patients who have no conscious memory of a word list can pick out the list from memory with stem completions (when given just the first three letters). For a good review of the literature regarding this finding, read *Implicit Learning and Tacit Knowledge* by Arthur Reber (1993).

Transfer

While there is limited learning transfer in explicit techniques (does knowing names, places, facts, and formulas really help outside of a test?), there is evidence of considerable transfer with implicit learning (Manza and Reber 1992).

Integrative

Implicit learning is powerful because it acts as a bridge between the body and mind. Dr. Robert Malmo at McGill University has researched the mind-body link as it applies to implicit learning. His conclusion after thirty years of study is that all thinking has a physical link (Hanna 1993). Using EEG monitors to record mental activity during a variety of experiments, researchers found that during cognitive activity, muscle tension varies dramatically depending on content and context (ibid). For example, listening to a story triggered muscular tension; telling a story engaged muscular tension; and getting praised or criticized impacted muscle tension. The bottom line here is that, even when you think you're doing something mental, it has a physical component and vice versa.

Now that you've read the rationale in support of more implicit learning strategies, tell me, can classroom lecturing stand up to the same kind of scrutiny? If you have discovered a strategy more effective than implicit learning, you ought to bottle it because, so far, implicit learning is the closest thing I believe we have to a magic formula!

Let's Review... 10 Reasons for Implicit Learning

1. Robustness
2. Independent of Age
3. Ease of Learning
4. Cross-Cultural Transmission
5. Independent of Intelligence
6. Efficiency
7. Value
8. Integrity
9. Transfer
10. Integrative

More Ways to Remember

Our brain possesses a hierarchy system, much like that of a well-organized office. The top priority concerning our brain is survival of the organism. Thus, all things related to our survival are easily stored and remembered, while the less meaningful information is given secondary status. We tend to remember best traumatic, painful, and pleasurable experiences. We remember where good food and water sources are; we retain important numbers; we master important motor skills like walking, talking, and running; and we learn how to read our environment. On the other hand, we are less efficient at remembering the kinds of things we typically test on in the traditional school setting. Such knowledge, which is typically pretty low on our survival scale, requires a great deal more effort on the part of our conscious brain. But there is a solution.

Emotional Stimuli Enhances Memory

By engaging the active memory pathways (the "how" and the "wow") of implicit learning, we create an additional "hook" for remembering the material. The strength of the synaptic connection is enhanced when movement (the "how" pathway) is engaged in conjunction with an emotive "binder" (the "wow" pathway), such as shock, fear, surprise, or excitement (Cahill, et al. 1994). Traditional seatwork engages less of the brain. If you want your learners to remember what they are learning, get them involved: Get them moving. Start "playing" more and "working" less.

Take the Long View of Play

Too often, due to time pressures, administrative pressures, and high-stakes testing, we forget to balance the long view with the short view. Will a learner be better off on any given day if he/she gets to play? It's unlikely, but over the long-term, working with our biological imperatives rather than against them makes a whole lot of sense. Why? Because movement, games, and play provide genuine value to both learning and survival.

Even ancient cultures recognized the value of play, games, and movement. We play because that's life's natural curriculum. It provides us with vital feedback in a nonthreatening way. When lion cubs play, they are acquiring hunting skills. Fish play and learn to escape predators. We play and learn to make a living. From playing house to doctor, teacher, and soldier, the games kids play are means for exploring the world's intricacies. And when enmeshed in such play, children have no ends in mind, no goals, no limitations (Wohlwill 1984). Acting out scenarios provides us with a means for learning without paying heavy penalties. Intrinsic learning thrives in an environment of low threat, high feedback, and big fun, where many chances to learn are inherent as opposed to test time when the stakes are high and the consequences for failure great.

While the consequences for mistakes at test time are heavy—maybe a bad grade, embarrassment, or loss of privileges—play allows us to learn quickly from our mistakes (a poor throw, a missed social cue, a step too slow, a confused set of directions, or an inappropriate comment, etc.) without lethal consequences.

Increase learning with minimal downside risk: From the point of view of learning, you can't beat play. The inverted U-shaped curve at right suggests that play maximizes the critical period during the selectively experience-dependent stage of synaptic elimination. This is occurring in all areas of the brain, but particularly in the neuron-packed cerebellum with the Purkinje cells, where fine motor output is delineated (Beyers 1998). Researchers say, "Animals and humans at play are motivated to repeat newly acquired skills in the absence of immediate external goals, thereby increasing the strength of neurological structures underlying these skills and opening opportunities for further learning (Byers and Walker 1995). In

U-Shaped Learning Curve

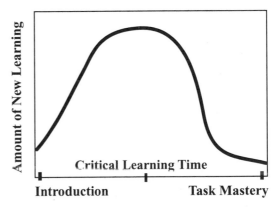

addition, imitation learning is a factor. If a child sees another doing something that gets the teacher's favored response, it may encourage the imitation of the behavior (Bandura 1977).

The renowned Russian psychologist Lev Vygotsky (1978) understood that play was a leading factor in a child's development. Play teaches socially and culturally appropriate ways of behaving among peers in a low-threat context as our own understanding of the world around us is shaped and reshaped. Play continues throughout life, and as we become parents and grandparents, the cycle is renewed. Making faces with an infant, playing peekaboo with a toddler, and doing somersaults with a preschooler serve to enhance the mechanisms for both cooperation and compromise, characteristics clearly of benefit to our species (Boulton and Smith 1992).

Adults go to amusement parks, celebrate with friends, dance the night away, dress up for Halloween, and play games from bingo to volleyball. Interestingly, such play does not stop as we age; it's just modified. Adult dogs still chase Frisbees; adult cats still chase balls. And, the games your four-year old may be playing now—puddle jumping, rope skipping, and make believe house—are the real-world activities of tomorrow.

The pleasure we derive from play can be a vehicle to better physical and mental health. Play allows us to take charge of events in our lives that may feel out of control. As we create imaginative scenarios (haunted houses, Marti Gras, and Halloween are classic examples), we conquer our fears. Children especially find release through their fantasies.

Play Enhances Brain Connections

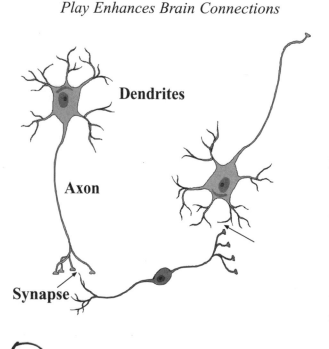

Dendrites

Axon

Synapse

Brain development may, in fact, be enhanced by play. In the early years of a child's development, the complex interaction of social, physical, and emotional factors contribute towards neural connectedness. Connectivity is a crucial feature of brain development because the neural pathways formed during the early years carry signals that allow us to process information throughout our lives (Dixon and Shore 1997). Play provides the vehicle for the countless interactions necessary between child and caregiver. The close, emotional attunement derived from play is critical to the healthy development of a child's brain (Gunnar 1996). In fact, one of the most powerful aspects of play is its ability to unite the developing areas of the brain (van Hoorn, et al. 1993). It helps orchestrate the intricate tuning of emotions, social skills, cognition, and motor development.

Play Enhances Learning

Cognition

Making predictions
Developing symbolic capacity
Comparing and contrasting
Enhancing literacy skills
Solving problems

Organizing a project
Practicing newly acquired skills
Attempting novel or complex tasks
Developing a better understanding of time
Drawing conclusions

Creativity

Extending ideas
Using new mediums for expression
Using rhythm, singing, and music
Improvising

Improvising ideas
Flexible thinking
Experimenting with "make-do" items

Healthy Lifestyle

Improving large/gross motor skills
Interpreting rules
Developing fine motor skills
Improving self-trust and competence

Learning safety precautions
Better use of outdoors
Learning nutrition concepts

Social Skills

Making and being a friend
Sharing and taking turns
Cooperation
Learning multiple roles

Understanding feelings
Conflict resolution
Becoming sensitive to other's feelings

Can you think of any other activity that facilitates so many important learning skills while integrating social, cognitive, and motor learning? From the constructivist view, which holds that we build and create our own realities through a continuing spiral of mental construction, play is the one best ways to develop the whole person. Play ought to be an essential part of teaching, say some (Bredekamp and Copple 1997). It's one of the more effective strategies for learning known.

Play is an avenue for youngsters and adolescents to "get into shape" (Pellegrini and Smith 1998a), an avenue of assimilation (process oriented), and an avenue for goal achievement. In education and training contexts, play has other important purposes, as well, including enhanced cognition, motivation, and memory.

So why then do some teachers disregard play as frivolous? Our attitudes about play are mixed and are heavily dependent upon the cultural norms of our experience in life, especially early on. Nevertheless, we all (with only extreme exceptions) had some play experiences by virtue of being human. As we continue to explore movement and play as a vehicle for effective learning, you may find your own attitude about play shifting. By redefining the value of all forms of movement in the teaching and learning process, many positive things start happening. Most of them you'd never predict!

Time for a Break!

Before enjoying this book any further, now is a good time to pause for a break. I would recommend that you do something active, like one of the following suggested activities, but NOT more reading. At least, not just yet.

✦ **Stand up and stretch for a minute.**

✦ **Go get a glass of water and rehydrate.**

✦ **Find a quick chore to do.**

✦ **Go for a five-minute walk.**

✦ **Put on music and dance.**

✦ **Reflect on your learning and take notes.**

✦ **Do some cross-lateral motions.**

After you've taken a brief break, then come back to the book. Remember, the power of learning means you have the capacity to change and integrate new information beginning immediately. So why not start a new habit right now. Let's embody the new learning before we try to effectively teach it to others. We learn the most through example, imitation, and role modeling.

Take the message of movement and begin applying it now. Remember, if you don't live it, you don't believe it.

CHAPTER TWO

The Moving Brain

Frequently I am asked, "Where in the brain does this or that occur?" The question is both critical and irrelevant at the same time. To say that a particular activity engages a specific part of the brain may be partly accurate. However, it would also be somewhat misleading in that it ignores the complexity of the systems involved and the uniqueness of learners. The better we understand the locations, constraints, and mechanisms of the particular areas of the brain involved in an activity, the better we can put the knowledge in context and apply it. But even so, brains are not hardwired Nintendo sets all built exactly the same and programmed for certain responses.

Our lobes are not like compartmentalized assembly-line workers, each doing their respective jobs while on shift and then going home to rest awhile. Rather, a better metaphor for the brain is a midsized city that never rests, where people move constantly from area to area, and where rapid transportation between main highways (arteries in the brain) or along side streets (veins in the brain) is the norm. The brain is quite a busy organ—not merely a business, but a network of businesses, a system of systems.

Movement: The Choreography of Systems

These powerful neurobiological systems begin development prior to birth but they shift into high gear when we enter the world. The massive exposure to sensory input begins the intricate connecting and massive pruning process necessary to make sense of our world. We begin with reflex movement and soon we are capable of thoughtful action. Later we can represent objects and then abstractions. However, this fast-developing system does not mature on its own. It requires work, or better yet, play! Our brain needs a huge amount of input and feedback from the real world to simultaneously develop the dozen, at least, complex systems that are required of the moving child. The bottom line is that most complex movements activate multiple systems, including the following:

- ✦ **Pleasure-and-Reward System** (basal ganglia, thalamus, etc.)
- ✦ **Fine- and Gross-Motor Movement Systems** (involving multiple lobes)
- ✦ **Sympathetic Stress Response System** (thalamus, pituitary, adrenals)
- ✦ **Circulatory and Neurovascular Systems** (bloodstream, arteries, veins)
- ✦ **Vestibulocochlear Balance System** (cochlea, vestibular, auditory nerve)

- **Immune System** (white blood cells and free radicals)
- **Attentional and Alarm Systems** (thalamus, amygdala, prefrontal cortex)
- **Visual System** (thalamus, occipital, optic nerve)
- **Sensory-Motor System** (parietal lobe, cerebellar, prefrontal cortex)
- **Cognitive Skills** (prefrontal cortex, cingulate gyrus)
- **Emotional/Social Attunement** (occipital lobe, amygdala, orbitofrontal lobes)
- **Memory Systems** (cerebellum, parietal lobe, amygdala, temporal lobe)

Brain and Muscle Movement Pathways

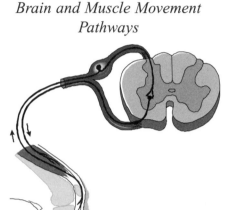

These multiple systems, which are engaged simultaneously and work in concert, have the complex job of first and foremost ensuring your survival. Your central nervous system, from the day you are born, is charged with modulating the other systems (cognition) based on experience and values (emotions) and the limitations of your body (ability) so that it can interact with environmental constraints (the world) to solve problems. In short, we can walk and gesture because we have learned how to assemble our thoughts and activate our gross- and fine-motor muscles in a way that allows us to successfully navigate our bodies, as well as the forces of gravity and social considerations, so we can interact. In short, you can't just act. You can't just move. You have to balance decision making, muscle movement, values, social considerations, and objectives every single split second. The graphic on this page illustrates the path between the brain's movement areas and the actual muscles involved.

Imagine a kid up to bat in Little League intent on hitting the ball or a child performing in a school play: Every single one of his or her twelve systems are engaged for the challenging task at hand. This complex engagement, and eventual enhancement, of our innate biological systems does not happen with seatwork; it only happens with activity. We are always creating an effect that involves our mind, our body, and the environment. Managing the constraints inherent in such activities requires complex cognitive behaviors, which get fine-tuned with practice.

Here's an interesting way of thinking about thinking: Thoughts are simply movements that haven't happened yet (and they might never happen!). Credit for this insight goes to University of Washington neurophysiologist William Calvin (1996), who has studied the relationship between movement and thinking. Whereas picking up a pencil or pen requires little advance planning, throwing a playground ball requires a great deal of neural planning because you are moving too fast to make the corrections once you start. In fact, Calvin says, just to throw an object twice as far, requires sixty-four times as many neurons. To throw something three times as far requires 729 times as many neurons, so they must recruit helpers for the more difficult task (ibid). Movement requires a great deal of our brain for many reasons; planning is just one of them.

Some early studies identified the motor cortex in the parietal lobe and the cerebellum as responsible for movement, but we now know that most of the brain is activated during physical activity. In his revolutionary book, *The Cognitive Neuroscience of Action*, Marc Jeannerod (1997) defines what it means to be physically and mentally active. We now know that intelligence is not merely a mental phenomenon and that the mind cannot be educated without the participation of the body, he says. This revolutionary research flies in the face of the old style education theory. A huge amount of trial-and-error learning happens with the interplay of the frontal and parietal lobes and the cerebellum. Breathing, muscle control, posture, heart rate, and countless decisions allow us to learn. The body "frames" the learning context for the mind. It's no longer mind *or* body: We now know it is the complex interplay between mind *and* body that engages the learning brain.

You've probably heard the old adage that we commonly use only 5 to 10 percent of our brain. Well, this claim may be vastly overstated. Mark Hallet, chief neurologist of the human motor control section for neurological disorders and stroke at the National Institutes of Health, estimates that when one achieves excellence in a sport, they are probably using close to 100 percent of their brain (Hallet 1999). "High levels of achievement in purely physical skills follow the same developmental course observed among highly successful mathematicians, sculptors, and research scientists," he adds. The take home message here is that the outdated perception of separateness between mind and body is an illusion: Complex interactions and movements require much more.

How Our Systems Are Activated

Each system is activated by its own "triggers." For example, our attentional system is activated by movement, contrast, and shape. Our auditory system responds only to a certain range of frequencies below 20,000 hertz. Our emotional system responds to both subtle emotions (orbitofrontal cortex) and intense emotions (amygdala). But the old myth of body learning as a spot in the brain allocated only to sensations or movement is outdated. There is a significant body of research that has linked the area of the brain long thought to be dedicated to "body-learning," the cerebellum, with cognitive processes, as well (Parsons and Fox 1997; Gao, et al 1996). This makes intuitive sense, but the metaphor needs to be even larger. It is not mind and body; it's rather mind, body, *and environment* that impact our vast biological system.

The intricacies of the following dozen neurobiological systems become even more intricate when skill level, age, and developmental stages are factored in. Suffice it to say that the brain is a system of systems and a strong kinetic program intensifies their coordinated activation. Let's take a look, however, at a synopsis of each system separately before examining the interplay between them.

Our Key Biological Systems

Our Pleasure-and-Reward System:

The commonly touted "reward circuit" was first described by scientists studying the reaction of the brain to "pleasure drugs." Starting near the top of the brainstem, the ventral tegmental area (VTA) projects towards the nucleus accumbens, then on to the prefrontal cortex. Our neurotransmitter of pleasure ("gotta have it") is dopamine. It's produced at the top of the brainstem. When released by the axon, dopamine molecules bind to the appropriate dopamine receptor sites on the connecting dendrite. Neighboring neurons release endorphins that bind to opiate receptors. Then, a split second later, excess dopamine is reabsorbed, excess endorphins are destroyed by enzymes, and the process repeats itself.

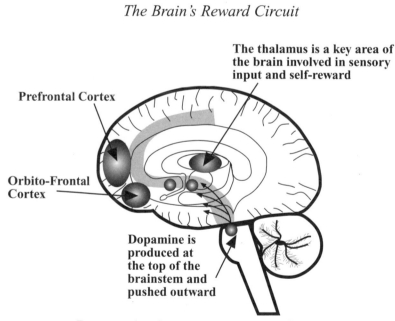

The Brain's Reward Circuit

The thalamus is a key area of the brain involved in sensory input and self-reward

Prefrontal Cortex

Orbito-Frontal Cortex

Dopamine is produced at the top of the brainstem and pushed outward

Receptor sites for the molecules that trigger pleasure are distributed throughout the body but are concentrated here in this "reward circuit."

This same system is activated by anything that's fun, which can include unfortunately things that are dangerous, like drugs, nicotine, and thrill seeking. It also, however, includes celebrations, falling in love, sexual pleasure, and a host of social rewards. In addition, there are also projections (axons) from the cerebellum to the midbrain areas that elicit pleasure. This may be nature's way of ensuring we enjoy the play process. When play activates a pleasurable memory or prior learning, the amygdala, the part of our brain that seems to store emotionally-intense memories, may also be implicated.

Fine- and Gross-Motor Movement System:

Our fine-motor systems are highly represented in our parietal lobes. Nature has allocated a hugely disproportionate amount of neural space for our hands and feet. This suggests that these are quite important to our species, and our survival does, in fact, depend mostly on the use of our hands, feet, and face, which enable us to communicate, find food, and eat. But our face also enables us to act and read. We have a large representation for our hands to fashion tools, but we can also catch, throw, hold, spin, rock, mold, sculpt, and draw. We have a large representation for our legs and feet, as well, enabling us to hunt, dance, run, play sports, and drive. This part of the brain is critical: "...it instructs us that human beings do not simply function as mouths that forage for themselves; we are also language users who communicate, and tool makers who construct" (Hanna 1993). In short, our brain is designed for moving, not sitting.

Fine Motor Pathways

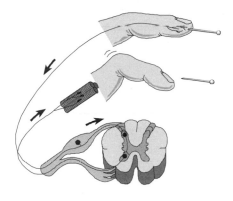

Nobel laureate Roger Sperry (1968) says "the entire output of our thinking mechanism goes into the motor system." Your brain creates movements by sending a deluge of nerve impulses to the appropriate muscles. And each movement, in turn, activates cortical areas. Since each specific muscle has to get the message at a slightly different time, it's a bit like a well-timed explosion on a special effects team. That amazing brain-body sequence is often referred to as a spatiotemporal (space-time) pattern, or simply a cerebral code (Calvin 1996).

Stress Response System

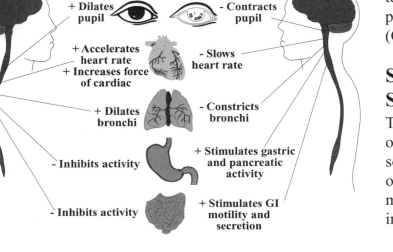

Sympathetic Nerves

Parasympathetic Nerves

+ Dilates pupil
- Contracts pupil
+ Accelerates heart rate
+ Increases force of cardiac
- Slows heart rate
+ Dilates bronchi
- Constricts bronchi
- Inhibits activity
+ Stimulates gastric and pancreatic activity
- Inhibits activity
+ Stimulates GI motility and secretion

Sympathetic Stress Response System:

This system is as important as any to our health and well-being. Daily stressors have only mild to moderate impact on this system, but when they become moderate to strong, this system jumps into action. The hypothalamus, our thermostat for change, is where the stress response originates. It produces corticotropin releasing factor (CRF) to the pituitary gland, which releases adrenocorticotropic hormone (ACTH) into the bloodstream. Within seconds, it arrives at the adrenal glands, which then secrete glucocorticoids and norepinephrine to help us deal with the stressors. Occasional release of these glucocorticoids in our system is not problematic; however, prolonged exposure to them can cause cognitive deficits. Activity and exercise can, however, reduce the blood levels of these hormones.

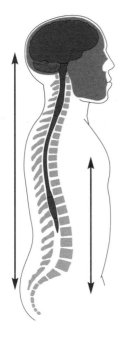

Circulatory and Neurovascular Systems:

Exercise, play, and activity are natural stimulants to this massive system. In healthy amounts, cognition and other areas are enhanced through activation of this system, which works parasynaptically, meaning "outside of the synapse." Thus, information does not have to take the usual neuron-to-neuron pathway (axons, synapses and dendrites), but can take the mass transit equivalent of a subway or the Concorde. Brain information is in transit through your body all the time. Former National Institute of Health neuroscientist Miles Herkenham believes that this system, which stores and transmits parasynaptic information in the body, transports 98 percent of all the brain's information!

The carrier of this parasynaptic messenger takes the form of a ligand. These are information carrying molecules, most commonly peptides (chained amino acids), that circulate throughout the body in your bloodstream and relay information. They find and lock onto their target receptor sites, much like a car looking for a parking space with its name on it. When they find the right site, they dock and transmit the information.

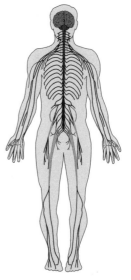

What does this mean to you? Bits of information from your brain are circulating throughout your body all the time! They share so much of the same common information that we can say they are one. But why is this significant?

If information transfer does not usually take the so-called normal pathways of learning, maybe we are making some incorrect assumptions about teaching. Maybe the way people learn best is not the formal, didactic, direct instruction approach in which we learn the facts, code them through synapses, and then repeat the process in hope of remembering them. Maybe we learn best when the information is stored in our body and embedded in emotions and context.

Neuroscientist Candace Pert (1997) of Georgetown Medical Center says that emotions, in fact, are not located in one specific area of the brain, but the receptor sites for them are dispersed throughout the brain and body. She calls the whole body the vehicle for our nonconscious mind. Implicit learning bypasses the usual neuron-to-neuron connection and is stored in the body. Suddenly movement education takes on whole new meaning.

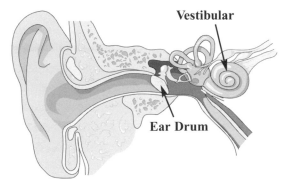

Auditory Pathways

Vestibular

Ear Drum

Vestibulocochlear Balance System:

This system, which is next to the inner ear and encompasses the auditory system, is one of the most critical for cognition. It is, in fact, the first sensory system to fully develop. The vestibular nuclei are closely modulated by the cerebellum, parietal lobes (sensory cortex), auditory nerves, and frontal lobes. This interaction helps us keep our balance, turn thinking into actions, and coordinate moves. This helps explain the value in playground games that stimulate inner ear motion like swinging, spinning, rolling, jumping, and turning. What the developing brain needs for successful movement and cognitive growth is sufficient activation of this motor-cellebellar-vestibular system. Without it, problems in learning can arise, which include attentional deficits, reading problems, emotional disregulation, weak memory skills, slow reflexes, lack of impulse control, and impaired or delayed writing skills.

This amazing system, which maintains both our stationary and movement orientations on a visual, auditory, and kinesthetic level, is critical for coping, thriving, and learning. Approximately one-fifth of all visual messages are used in this system for balance and stabilization. Think of all the things you see and do while moving your head. Or think of how well you keep your head stable while moving! Three bony semicircular canals help you maintain this balance. The endolymph fluid in these ducts flows over hair cells that are activated and send messages that allow you to make corrections in your movements. Without this incredibly efficient cognitive gyroscope you would not be able to perform simple daily tasks like mowing the lawn or enjoy such simple pleasures as taking a walk.

If you use the myelination of axons as a benchmark of cortical maturation, you can measure the rate of growth. This can be compared against a series of sensory inputs as well as feedback mechanisms. Greater maturation, as well as other indicators, contribute to cognitive precursors in the first few years. The vestibular area of the brain contributes the greatest proportion of essential stimuli and subsequent maturation compared to any other type of sensory input. Thus, spinning, tumbling, and rolling motions are great for the developing brain. Add to this tactile, pressure, and passive movements and you have more than 50 percent of all sensory input accounted for. Gross-motor movement has a special and critical role in the development of this essential system (Norton 1970).

Early indicators of the potential for spinning vestibular stimulation activities were derived mostly from animal models. Rats that were spun for just three minutes a day were superior to others in maze learning (Young 1964). Later human studies confirmed benefits from a training program that emphasized vestibular stimulation (Palmer 1980). For years sensory motor activists/researchers, like Jean Ayers, Moshe Feldenkrais, Glen Doman, Lyelle Palmer, and Carla Hannaford, have outlined the pathways and benefits of a full vestibular stimulation program.

Immune System:

Our immune system is dependent upon many factors for maximum effectiveness. These include smart lifestyle choices, avoidance of toxins, good nutrition, stress management, and of course, physical activity. Proper nutrition enhances our defenses against the free radicals that are highly detrimental to our health. Recent models suggest that our immune system is highly sensitive to oxygenation, distress, and heart rate. Specialized protection cells, known as NK cells, protect the body from health threats. Changes in the body's number of these NK cells is, in fact, a benchmark of overall health and well-being. Our immune system is highly responsive to distress—especially chronic stress. Even the stress of loneliness and heartbreak can lower the number of active NK cells in normal populations, emphasizing the value of social support, meditation, and relaxation strategies as part of a good school health program. In addition, good activity programs that include vigorous workouts will enhance this system, as well.

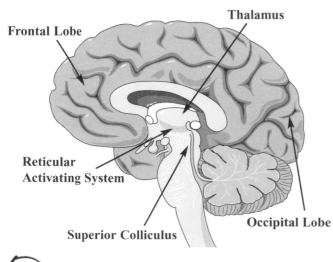

Areas Involved in Getting and Keeping Attention

Frontal Lobe

Thalamus

Reticular Activating System

Superior Colliculus

Occipital Lobe

Attentional and Alarm Systems:

Getting and keeping our attention requires activating multiple areas of the brain. Initially, we activate the thalamus and reticular activating system (RAS) near the top of the brainstem—an area that regulates incoming sensory data. Here our brain sorts the visual, auditory, and kinesthetic information at high speeds, carefully deciding if any of it contains life-threatening consequences. The better tuned this system, the safer we are and the more competence we can achieve.

Physical activity tunes this system through the attentional demands of sports, play, recess, performance, and games. Requiring persistent vigilance and rapid responses to external stimuli, such activity places heavy demands on our attentional systems. An emphasis on getting into "the zone" for maximum performance is healthy as the benefits spill over to other cognitive domains, as well.

Visual Systems:

The human visual system, which is quite important to our movement activities, develops in synchrony with our motor areas, suggesting a strong dependence on each other. Each eye sends information to contralateral hemispheres for processing. Researchers have identified greater than thirty layers in the visual system allowing us to process not only color and shape, but depth, motion, contrast, and other intricacies, as well. Neurons project from the premotor area—located in the lower parietal lobe—to the spinal cord suggesting that physical action maintains an integral relationship with our sensory system. Neurons in this area that respond to watching a task are called "mirror neurons" because they assist in imitation learning.

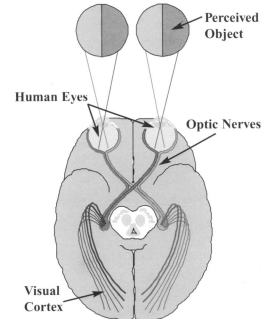

Visual Pathways

Perceived Object

Human Eyes

Optic Nerves

Visual Cortex

Our visual system is also instrumental in detecting social cues. But it cannot do it by itself. It takes the frontal lobes to interpret the data, unless the frontal lobes are immature. Normally, the frontal lobes mature between the ages of sixteen and twenty. This means that adolescents are typically inept at interpreting social cues. Instead, they are more likely to overreact, using their amygdala, a structure involved in intense emotions. This helps explain why there are so many social and emotional upsets among teens. They are simply not good yet at reading other people's emotional states.

Sensory-Motor System:

We have three types of neurons—sensory, intermediate, and motor. Our sensory motor system is designed to act on our thoughts through a dynamic interplay of brain areas. Some of our sensory neurons are almost three feet long! This allows them to be present in the brain and still stimulate areas far away. In order to be able to move smoothly, we integrate multiple brain sites.

Sensory Areas in the Brain

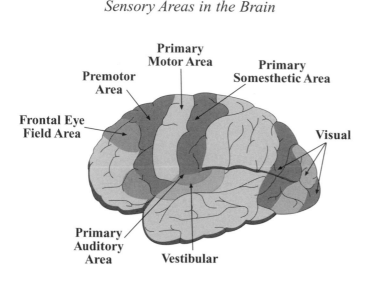

Primary Motor Area

Primary Somesthetic Area

Premotor Area

Frontal Eye Field Area

Visual

Primary Auditory Area

Vestibular

Located at the base of the brain, the cerebellum (Latin for "little brain") contains about 40 percent of the brain's neurons. The cerebellum, long thought of as necessary for posture and movement, also detects signals from the spinal column (results of movement) and compares them with signals from the parietal and frontal lobes (intentions) to make corrections. And for many years, it was assumed that input from the volitional brain was sent to the cerebellum to carry out the task. We now know that there are more neurons with axons that leave the cerebellum, communicating with other parts of the brain, than the reverse. This suggests that the cerebellum (our movement-maker) does not passively wait for a command, but rather actively participates in our lives. There's also a pathway from the cerebellum back to parts of the brain involved in memory, attention, and spatial perception. Amazingly, the part of the brain that processes movement is the same part of the brain that processes learning.

Cognitive System:

The frontal lobes are known as the executive or master decision-makers of our brain. Over the past decade, we have identified pathways that travel from the cerebellum to brain areas involved with attention, memory, spatial guidance, rhythm, perception, and body positioning. This suggests that it's not just our conscious mind telling our "brain's engine" what to do, but the reverse is also true.

This part of the brain is critical for filtering and integrating the massive stream of incoming sensory data enabling us to make wise decisions about what to do and how to do it. Let's say, for example, that you put in a long day at work and

Cognitive Systems

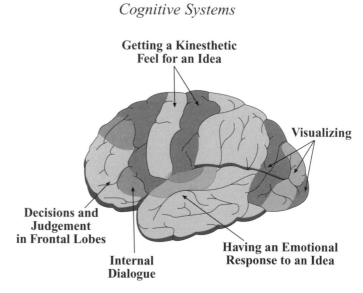

Getting a Kinesthetic Feel for an Idea

Visualizing

Decisions and Judgement in Frontal Lobes

Internal Dialogue

Having an Emotional Response to an Idea

now you're relaxing in your lounge chair at home with a margarita. Your spouse asks if you want to go out dancing, since you mentioned earlier in the week that, as a couple, you hadn't gone out for awhile. You might intellectually feel like you want to go dancing, but your body feels like resting. Typically, how the body feels wins out over how the head feels. In this case, body rules mind, and you say, "No thanks."

Emotional/Social Attunement System:

This system enables us to manage our approach and avoidance behaviors. When we are in tune with others, we are more likely to approach them wisely. This is commonly a left-hemisphere activity; however, the right hemisphere is activated, as well, especially during avoidance. The area of the brain involved with attunement is the orbitofrontal cortex, located in the lower frontal lobes just behind the eyes. This area allows us to integrate our feelings with environmental sensations and cognition to help us make wise decisions.

Memory Systems:

Different kinds of memories are distributed in different areas of the brain. For example, we now know that the instructions for performing a particular task are well distributed throughout the brain. Memory for sequence and order of physical actions (i.e., first you plug in the vacuum, then you turn it on, then you push) is stored in the motor cortex. The cerebellum, which has long been recognized as responsible for more than gross-motor movement and posture, is thought now to be involved with cognition, behavior, anticipation, analysis, and execution (Gao, et al. 1996; Parsons and Fox 1997).

Location of Memory Systems

Amygdala
(mediates intense emotional events)

Cortex
Temporal lobes
(semantic retrieval)

Hippocampus
(mediates semantic & episodic memory)

Parietal
Lateral intraparietal
(short-term memory)

Prefrontal Cortex
(short-term memory)

Cerebellum
(prodedural learning, reflexive learning, & conditioned responses)

Body Memories
Peptide molecules circulate throughout the entire body via the bloodstream

Our memories of intense emotional events, whether active or not, are stored in the amygdala. Visual memories are stored in the visual cortex (occipital lobe), and short-term memories are probably stored in the frontal lobes.

Interaction Patterns

I've introduced these systems as if they are separate for the sake of clarity; they are not, however. They cannot and do not operate in a vacuum. Nearly every action, from an approach behavior (meeting a new person or pouring a cup of coffee) to building a model or playing a piano involves delicate interplays among these systems. In summary, the original question, "Where in the brain does this or that occur?" is complex. The short answer, however, is "Everywhere!" The long answer, I'm afraid, is the topic for another book. For a more in-depth analysis of the subject, I recommend *Images of Mind* by Michael Posner and Marcus Raichle (1994) and *The Cognitive Neuroscience of Action* by Marc Jeannerod (1997). Now that we've established that implicit learning is a powerful mechanism for learning, and that most of the brain is involved in active learning, let's explore the how and the why of movement in learning.

Time for a Break!

Before enjoying this book any further, now is a good time to pause for a break. I would recommend that you do something active, like one of the following suggested activities, but NOT more reading. At least, not just yet.

✦ **Stand up and stretch for a minute.**

✦ **Go get a glass of water and rehydrate.**

✦ **Find a quick chore to do.**

✦ **Go for a five-minute walk.**

✦ **Put on music and dance.**

✦ **Reflect on your learning and take notes.**

✦ **Do some cross-lateral motions.**

After you've taken a brief break, then come back to the book. Remember, the power of learning means you have the capacity to change and integrate new information beginning immediately. So why not start a new habit right now. Let's embody the new learning before we try to effectively teach it to others. We learn the most through example, imitation, and role modeling.

Take the message of movement and begin applying it now. Remember, if you don't live it, you don't believe it.

CHAPTER THREE

Indoor Games

When using indoor games for educational objectives, it is important not to make the assumption that any kind of game is appropriate. Silly, confusing activities without a clear purpose are time wasters. Indoor games and movement activities, however, that are aligned with learning goals, presented at an appropriate challenge level, that are safe, relevant, fun, and inclusive of all learners, maximize learning efficiency. In addition, the rules of the activity need to be clearly stated, understood, and agreed upon to avoid potential feelings of failure, confusion, or embarrassment. And, learners should have ample opportunities for feedback and correction during the process.

At the K-5 level, activities should be brief in duration. As a general rule, a purposely planned activity lasting approximately ten minutes of every learning hour helps students maintain a productive mind-body state. Providing two recesses thirty minutes each in duration, in addition to the frequent classroom movement activities, is optimal. If two short recesses are not possible, one forty-five to sixty-minute recess is a good alternative.

At the secondary and adult level, continue to use these activities but with longer duration if desired. Follow the same general guidelines as those for K-5. This chapter includes, but is not limited to, energizers, stretching, breathing activities, games, and relays that can be conducted indoors.

What the Science Says

There are multiple good reasons to incorporate regular physical activity and movement into your lesson plans. Here are five: First, movement increases heart rate and subsequent circulation, therefore, arousal. Studies show increased performance following arousal activities (Tomporowski and Ellis 1986). In addition, increased arousal tends to narrow attention to target tasks (Easterbrook 1959). Stretching, which increases the cerebrospinal fluid flow to critical areas, is an example of a productive movement activity. While it increases oxygen to key brain areas, stretching also provides an opportunity for the eyes and musculo-skeletal system to relax (Henning, et al. 1997).

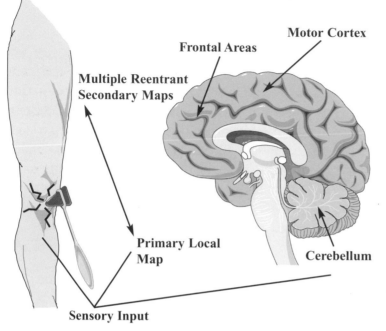

The Body's Response to Sensory Input

Frontal Areas

Motor Cortex

Multiple Reentrant Secondary Maps

Primary Local Map

Cerebellum

Sensory Input

Second, animal studies suggest that activity enhances spatial learning (Fordyce and Wehner 1993). At the very least, movement gives learners a different spatial perspective. This "fresh view" can enliven the senses and engage additional episodic memory "identifiers." In other words, new scenery can positively influence recall. How? Our brain forms maps, based not only on the scenery, but on our body's relationship to that scenery. Therefore, the room doesn't have to be new if the relationship between you and your position in a room or other location is different (Rizzolatti, et al. 1997). In my own one-day staff-development workshops, I always have participants move to a different side of the room after lunch. This keeps the audience seeing from a "novel" and uncontaminated "point of view."

Third, the principle known as "state-dependency" tells us that every physical, emotional, and cognitive state is comprised of a different rhythm in the brain, and that these oscillating rhythms originating in the thalamus trigger cues that activate a certain set of corresponding memories related to prior learning. This phenomenon is illustrated by the following scenarios:

1. *Have you ever noticed that when you're really mad at someone you can't remember anything they've ever done right?*

2. *Have you ever thought of something you wanted from another room in your house, but by the time you get there you can't remember what it was?*

3. *Have you ever noticed that when you're feeling positive about someone, you can't recall anything they've ever done poorly?*

4. *Have you ever noticed that when someone asks you how to do something, it's easier to recall if you go through the motions?*

First we have to have the knowledge, then we have to be able to recover it in order for it to be helpful. If state-dependency theory holds true, practicing the learning in multiple states of mind may develop greater cognitive flexibility and recall.

Fourth, breaking up the stream of content (sometimes referred to as spaced interval learning) with well distributed physical practice is far more effective than excessive content dumping. Some evidence points to the prudent use of spaced intervals in Japanese and Taiwanese schools as one explanation for their effective implementation of a longer, yet more productive learning day. Hence, even though the learning day is quite long, the spaced interval approach results in actually less content delivery than their Minneapolis counterpart (Stevenson and Lee 1990). While it may be the spaced intervals that are key here, it is also plausible that the type of play used to reinforce the learning may be instrumental in the success of these schools. As one researcher put it, "It remains questionable whether it is exercise/play per se, or rather the breaks from sustained classroom work, that are responsible for any increased cognitive performance" (Pellegrini and Smith 1998b).

Finally, certain kinds of movements can stimulate the release of the body's natural motivators. These chemical messengers, known as neurotransmitters, play a primary role in our mind-body states and receptivity to learning. If the activity is compelling, for example, noradrenaline (adrenaline) will be released; whereas, dopamine will be the likely agent if the activity involves the pleasure of social bonding, celebrations, rewards, or repetitive gross-motor movements. This is why "energizers" or quick little wake-up activities increase energy levels, improve storage and retrieval of information, and help learners feel good. Very short breaks or energizers increase arousal, but longer ones allow learners to reach a plateau state that may be more sustainable. However, either approach will work.

Release of Adrenaline

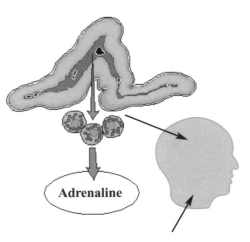

Adrenaline

"Chair-Man" of the Bored

While learning can be accomplished in sedentary fashion, it turns out that the typical notion of keeping students in chairs for extended periods of time may be misguided. The human body for the past fifty-thousand years has walked, run, skipped, or squatted, but it has not sat in chairs. Although our bodies have adapted somewhat to sitting in the relatively new innovation of chairs, we are historically more adept in

Improper Seating Posture

other positions. Sitting for long periods takes its toll on our body: In fact, spinal disc pressure is 30 percent greater when sitting versus standing (Zacharkow 1988) and results in the following risks: 1) poor breathing; 2) spinal column and lower back dysfunction; 3) poor eyesight; 4) overall body fatigue; and 5) less opportunity for implicit learning.

When we consider how much energy is used to maintain a posture that is ergonomically disadvantageous, we understand why we need to make the health of our body a learning priority. "Sitting in chairs for more than brief ten-minute intervals reduces our awareness of physical and emotional sensations" (Cranz 1998) and increases fatigue. These problems reduce concentration and attention, and ultimately result in discipline problems. However, when the core problem—sedentary lesson planning—is addressed, simple changes can be implemented for dramatic improvement.

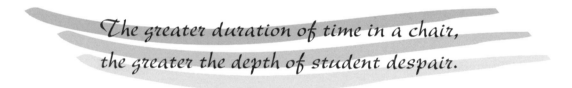

The greater duration of time in a chair, the greater the depth of student despair.

In fact, interestingly a German researcher found that the typical office worker (chair-sitter), whose "seat-time" equaled that of the typical student, had more musculo-skeletal problems than any other industry sector (Hettinger 1985). This conclusion is startling: Sitting is as much an occupational risk as lifting heavy materials, for instance, in a construction job. Clearly, the chairs we continue to use in schools do not offer enough flexibility to optimize learning (Rittel and Webber 1973). But this complaint is not new. As far back as 1912, Dr. Maria Montessori described the impact of chairs: "Children were not disciplined (when chairs were used), but annihilated"(Benton 1986).

The two postures that most aggravate back pain are stooping and sitting (Reisbrod and Greenland 1985). When subjects were asked to stoop, 60 percent experienced increased back pain, while 30 percent experienced a similar response to sitting. School children are generally subjected to both stooping and sitting for lengthy periods of time.

Another noted concern relative to seatwork is that while children's average height has continued to increase over the past few decades, school chair manufacturers have not altered their design specifications. And, while children's visual focus distance is less than that of adults (averaging 12 inches), children often compensate by leaning forward, rounding their backs, and ultimately creating strain. Such sitting postures put more pressure on the diaphragm and internal organs, restricting function, reducing blood circulation and oxygen to the brain, and increasing fatigue (Grimsrud 1990). In fact, the Director of the Institute of Occupational Health in Milan, Italy, said, "...holding any posture for long periods of time is the ultimate problem, but holding the classic right-angle seated posture, in particular, has its special stresses, which no amount of ergonomic tinkering can eliminate" (Grieco 1986).

Math teachers should have kids move in the same way D.E. teachers have kids count.

Is there a solution? Yes, there are a few simple remedies: First, teachers need to engage students in a wider variety of postures including walking, laying down, swinging, spinning, skipping, leaning, perching, kneeling, and squatting, while also providing learners with more movement choices throughout the day. One-third of all subjects with back pain (from prolonged stooping) experienced relief with walking (Biering-Sorensen 1984); yet, many teachers commonly ignore this simple "intervention."

In addition, providing ergonomically-correct chairs for learners can make a huge difference. Dr. A. Mandal, a Danish physician, says that the secret to healthy sitting is understanding the relationship between the legs and the spine (Mandal 1981). When that angle is between 120 and 135 degrees, halfway between sitting and standing, there's no uneven pressure on the body, he says. This posture provides more balance between the front and back pelvis muscles.

In addition to ergonomically-correct chairs, research suggests that subjects with slanted desks versus flat ones also experience less of the painful electromyogram activity in the lower back (Eastman and Kamon 1976). Slanted desks, it seems, translate to less fatigue (better concentration) and less eye strain (better reading). But even if your school can't or won't invest in new chairs and desks, most seated learning activities can be accomplished in alternate positions such as standing, leaning, squatting, kneeling, walking, or lying down.

Ultimately, a classroom where learning (rather than control) is the priority reveals a few distinct differences. First, the teachers regularly incorporate active learning and movement activities, and, second, they build flexibility into their lesson planning so that learners have posture choices and the freedom to move as their mind-body states require. Lastly, the most dedicated teachers argue for more ergonomically-correct classroom furniture.

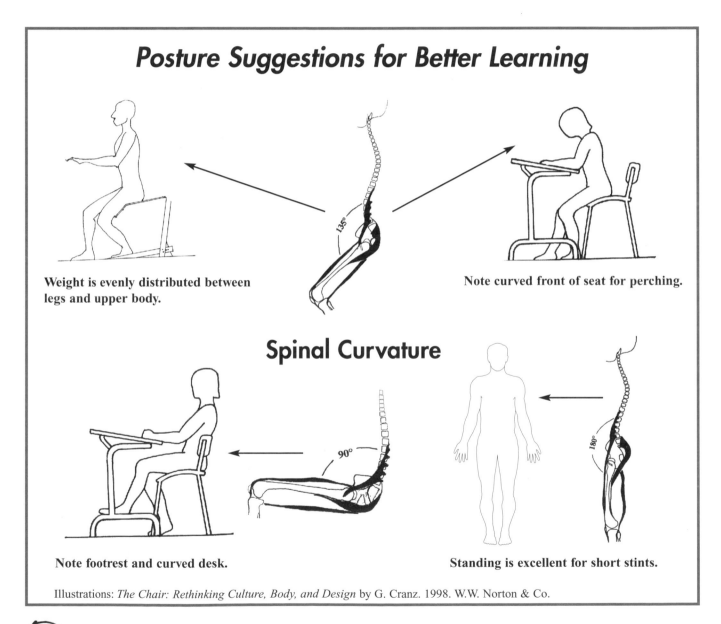

Posture Suggestions for Better Learning

Weight is evenly distributed between legs and upper body.

135°

Note curved front of seat for perching.

Spinal Curvature

Note footrest and curved desk.

90°

180°

Standing is excellent for short stints.

Illustrations: *The Chair: Rethinking Culture, Body, and Design* by G. Cranz. 1998. W.W. Norton & Co.

Perceptual-Motor/Cognition Enhancement

As far back as the early 1950s, Piaget (1952) proposed that children create and learn about the world through play. In fact, it is through play that children best explore their physical and emotional worlds, discover insights, create hypotheses, and experiment with their newfound knowledge. Two of the many important by-products of play are adaptive learning and pleasure. All of us know the importance of crawling, scooting, and rolling to infant development, but did you know that babies who do *not* crawl are probably *not* at risk for developing learning difficulties, assuming other milestones and behaviors are on track? And second, infants don't have a clearly defined transition stage from motor development to cognitive development. These developmental periods are, in fact, so intertwined, that each movement increases perception, which increases cognitive capabilities (Bushnell and Boudreau 1993). Ultimately, every movement baby makes contributes to his/her cognitive map.

When infants are given additional locomotor experience and older children are given locomotion training, their spatial search skills improve significantly (Kermoian and Campos 1988; Yan, et al. 1998). Thus, it makes good sense to encourage more "playground-type" interaction and movement activities, especially in the early elementary and preschool years. A complete routine would include movements such as spinning, crawling, rolling, rocking, tumbling, pointing, and matching. Dr. Lyelle Palmer of Winona State University has documented significant gains in attention and reading subsequent to interventions in which these stimulating activities are facilitated (Palmer 1980).

While it makes intuitive sense that children ought to play, challenge their gross-motor muscles, and have fun at it, there is compelling evidence that Piaget was right in saying, "A child's work is his play." Palmer's work, presented in a video instruction program co-written by him and myself (1995), called Bright Brain, is a highly beneficial method for preparing children for learning.

Movement's Impact on Learning

Another beneficial movement methodology, known as Educational Kinesiology (EK) or "Brain Gym," consists of a series of simple physical movements and positions in which the teacher asks children to follow along. This directed-movement program, which is currently used in thirty-six countries around the world, is often recommended for individuals with mild learning difficulties and behavior disorders. The founders of educational kinesiology, Dr. Paul and Gail Dennison (1989) cautiously understate, "Promise nothing; better to be surprised." However, both have excellent educational credentials and have promoted Brain Gym for years.

The Dennisons describe brain functioning in three simple dimensions: laterality (left and right hemisphere), focus (coordination between the front and back of the brain), and centering (coordination between the top and bottom of the brain). While this approach has not been peer reviewed or university supported, many advocates of the methodology have been effusive in its benefits. Studies have been conducted that support their work, but mostly with small samples and not longitudinal in nature. In addition, subjects haven't been tested for many of the potential disorders in advance; rather, reading scores are typically the primary measure.

Cross Crawl Activity

The cross crawl is an exercise in which movements are coordinated so that when one arm moves, the opposite leg moves. Ideal warm-ups require crossing the body's lateral midline. This activity activates the brain for crossing the visual/auditory /kinesthetic/tactile midline. It also improves coordination, spatial awareness, breathing, and stamina.

So, how much value is there in educational kinesiology? If children don't gain basic perceptual motor skills during early critical periods, can they still be obtained later? The answer seems to be yes, to a particular degree, anyway. In one survey of 180 controlled studies, the time invested in eye-hand coordination, balance, and motor skills suggested learning benefits, but not commensurate with time invested (Kavale and Mattson 1983). There are ambiguous links to academic performance when taught later (after age six), though there may be other benefits that are unable to be measured. Many of the studies that demonstrate the value in these types of activities have weak or no controls. It turns out that EK is tough to study because of the strong teacher involvement, making blind, random, or controlled designs difficult to implement.

In one EK study, the school records of twenty-five students were used, each with a recorded diagnosis of a learning disability. Ages ranged from seven to seventeen, with a mean of thirteen years old. All the subjects were white and middle class; six were girls, and four were left handed. Unfortunately, no control group was used, and the study used tests from the previous year as a benchmark. During the one year Brain Gym intervention program, all students made gains in language, arithmetic, and reading. However, the gains were in line with expected gains for any additional year of schooling (Cammisa 1994). Practice and maturation may have contributed to the gains. "This study suggests the use of Educational Kinesiology may improve perceptual motor skills of learning disabled children...This study did not, however, clarify the role of Educational Kinesiology in relation to academic achievement," said the study's author, Kathryne Cammisa (ibid).

While the broad-based literature does not support claims of significant changes in academic skills, the EK improvements in perceptual motor-skills are reliable. Studies by Khalsa (1988) and Sifft and Khalsa

(1991) found improvements in static balance and response times, and both attributes may be helpful in an academic setting. No contraindications or negative effects are evidenced. There may be, however, a strong influence prescribed by the particular teacher or practitioner. In other words, there is the suggestion that students may be merely benefiting from the extra attention, which alone can enhance learning.

Daily High-Low Cycles

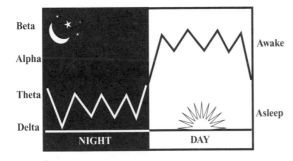

Waking Up the Brain

All of us typically have high and low energy cycles throughout the day occurring at 90- to 110-minute intervals. Controlled by our suprachiasmatic nucleus (SCN) near our thalamus and influenced by our hormones, high energy times occur approximately one-and-a-half hours after our last energy high, followed by a low energy time. In a typical class, some learners will be at the peak of their energy cycle, while others will be at the bottom. This rhythm also alternates in conjunction with left and right hemispheric efficiency. In other words, a learner will be more adept at sequential thinking and logic when the left hemisphere is dominant, followed forty-five minutes later by more random, creative, and spatial abilities when the right hemisphere is dominant. Neither is necessarily better than the other; it just depends on the task requirements at hand. But when learners get stuck, it may be that waiting an hour and trying again will get them unstuck. Movement activities can also help to re-balance learners who are too heavily weighted on one side of the brain or the other.

Recognizing the cyclical nature of our brains and bodies is one thing, but doing something about it is another. This is where classroom activities come in. Since the left hemisphere controls the right side of the body and the right hemisphere controls (to a degree, there is some dispute about this) the left side of the body, the bridge or link between these two hemispheres is important. Called the corpus callosum, this

bundle of 250 billion nerve fibers provides the "fiber optics" for each side to talk to the other. If you want to reduce the temporary lateralization in students (remember they may all be in different states at one time), you can facilitate exercises, known as cross-laterals, to create more cross-hemispheric activity.

A cross lateral is just that—an exercise whereby your left or right limb crosses over the visual field to the opposite side of the body (touching, for example, the right hand to the left knee or shoulder, etc). When a cross-lateral is performed, additional neural traffic allows the brain to sort out which side of the brain is now governing the anomaly (the left arm on the right side or vice versa). While there appears to be limited support for these movements in the technical research, the logic behind the exercises is compelling. The performance of a series of cross-laterals by learners does seem to stimulate and energize, but it's unknown whether it's purely an arousal effect or a real change in the type of stimulation to the brain. Additional studies need to be done in this area. Nevertheless, conducting about two to five minutes of cross-laterals certainly can't hurt, and probably will energize your learners. Try them for yourself! See cross-laterals on pages 43 and 95 and "Brainy Energizers" on page 110.

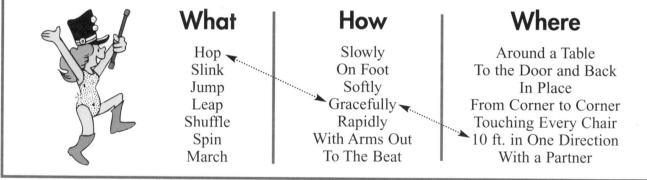

Movement Activities Made Easy

Simply add together lines from each of the "what," "how," and "where" columns below to form a host of action combinations. For example, "Hop gracefully ten feet in one direction" or "Jump rapidly in place."

What	How	Where
Hop	Slowly	Around a Table
Slink	On Foot	To the Door and Back
Jump	Softly	In Place
Leap	Gracefully	From Corner to Corner
Shuffle	Rapidly	Touching Every Chair
Spin	With Arms Out	10 ft. in One Direction
March	To The Beat	With a Partner

Sensory Integration

Sensory integration is another benefit of indoor play. Originally pioneered by Dr. Jean Ayers (1972, 1991), the methodology is now used by psychiatrists, occupational therapists, psychologists, and special education teachers. The theory behind it is that some children have difficulty registering and processing sensory information. Their "attentional engine" runs at an inappropriate level compared to other children in class. As a result, they exhibit "dysfunctional" focusing behaviors, which help them remain at their preferred level of arousal. For example, they may rock in their chairs, chew pencils, fidget with things, talk to themselves, and/or bounce around. Such behavior can be highly disruptive to the class, as well as detrimental to the student's own planning and learning. The unaware teacher may think these children are simply acting out for attention or are being impulsive, indolent, hypersensitive, and/or generally difficult out of spite. In fact, these learners are doing what comes quite naturally to their being.

When students misbehave, many "back-to-basics" conservatives say we just need more discipline in our schools. But brain disorders (especially in relation to the sensory system) are a common cause of behavior problems in students. Some estimate from 5 to 20 percent of all kids have sensory integration problems. Occupational therapists have known for decades that some children are hypersensitive to the visual, auditory, and tactile information most of us take for granted. Sensory disorders can make otherwise healthy kids seem clumsy, indolent, defensive, or hypersensitive. Simple events like a playground interaction, or even a wrinkled shirt, can trigger bizarre behaviors whereby the children destroy other kid's work, swear, run amok, or experience insomnia. Schools that have strong movement programs reduce the likelihood and severity of the condition. This whole concept of a dysfunctional nervous system in a child who otherwise displays normal to high functioning is perplexing to many educators. But remember, there is no fence between the mind and body.

Various programs have been developed to deal with the "fidgeting child." Many therapists use a specialized movement therapy to treat autism, learning disabilities, attentional deficits, and sensory-motor problems. The treatment, which varies from student to student, seems to work for many and usually involves a set of demanding exercises, play therapy designed to calm their nerves, and sometimes sound therapy. Prescription drugs are not ruled out, but used as a last resort. One student's routine consisted of trampoline play, rolling on a large fitness ball, chewing gum, and wearing a weighted vest to create a soothing weight on the body. Sound therapy often involves a combination of soothing tones from filtered music in which the listener must strain to hear certain pitches. One parent glowed, "Henry is sleeping better; his night terrors have stopped; and, academically, his reading skills and self-esteem have soared"(Chase 1999). All of these attributes hold a common denominator—they modulate the brain's sensory responses.

The Alert Program is one such program that helps students develop their own "engine speed" by identifying their sensory motor needs and providing more appropriate strategies including an "alert" box with items to help them cope. The coping "bag of tricks" might include brushes, gum, fidget toys, a kaleidoscope, blocks, lotion, or other items that potentially soothe them. Self-administered or therapist-administered treatments may involve specialized combinations of exercises, play-therapy, brushing the appendages to soothe the nerves, motor-skill practice, listening therapy, and weighted trainings where children wear a weighted vest and chew gum. There is no one secret to treat all children who are chaotic. Classroom activities which are narrow in focus and rhythmical may be the best for this child. It's best to refer any students who fit the profile to a resource specialist for optimal treatment. While the hard evidence on sensory integration identification and treatment is not compelling, many therapists have found paths to success with its use.

Emotional Expression

Many children today are coming to school with heavy concerns and problems and, increasingly, trauma. It's no longer a matter of *whether* they have major issues in their lives to face, but *when*. Many learners have them right now, today, as we speak, and many go unrecognized. The question we need to be asking is, "Am I recognizing them, or am I letting another kid fall through the cracks?" I know from personal experience that most teachers do not pick up on the cues that children give them. I was a victim myself, from the age of six to fifteen, of  physical childhood abuse, but not one of thirty-five teachers ever recognized the symptoms. I didn't expect my teachers to be therapists, but schools should be places where kids can express themselves and get help when they need it. Heavy emotional issues, such as mine, either get expressed or impair learning. In my case, I simply shut down and became difficult to reach. Play has been shown to be an excellent vehicle for the expression of emotions. Children with either expressive barriers or significant emotional "baggage" benefit the most from play acting (Carmichael and Atchinson 1997).

Many prominent researchers have suggested that emotional adaptation may be far more important to a child's success than cognitive skills (Goleman 1995). But when teachers feel so pressed for time, how do they find the resources to deal with this important learning dilemma? This is another powerful reason for the use of energizers, upbeat rituals, quick games, stretch breaks, and student-generated oxygenators. Games support the development of emotional intelligence in children while they facilitate face-to-face interactions, the management of feelings, the expression of verbal and nonverbal requests, the delaying of gratification, the use of self-talk, problem-solving, empathy, conflict resolution, and more. If you're not currently using games for emotional expression, what are you using instead?

Change of Body, Change of Mind

When teachers complain that students are not in a good state to learn, they should consider incorporating more movement into their lessons. Dr. Robert Thayer, who has researched mood regulation for twenty years, is adamant about the power of movement (Thayer 1996). He says, "The data suggest that exercise is the best overall mood regulator." Teachers who have learners sit too long, at any age, from pre-K through college level are missing the boat. When surveyed, students commonly suggest they use food and friends as a source of mood regulation. But Thayer suggests, aside from mandated vigorous exercise, that going for brisk walks are the single best way teachers can influence student's moods.

The Binding Solution

Another advantage derived from indoor play and movement activities is called "binding." This is the process whereby the brain links up information permanently, or binds one element to another. For example, how do we bind new vocabulary words with their definition in a context that is appropriately embedded with emotion? The answer is simple—our parents (or other caregivers) have raised us by teaching vocabulary words with enthusiasm, in a concrete, try-it-out way, followed by feedback (usually the rewards of cheers or smiles). This binding of cognition, emotion, meaning, and context works because it utilizes the elements of implicit learning: feelings, movement, and space. The content information alone is not enough to engage long-term memory. This is why savvy foreign language teachers incorporate role play, music, drama, emotions, simulations, and Total Physical Response (TPR). TPR is a method of instruction whereby foreign vocabulary words are taught in conjunction with movements. For example, the teacher would have students march, walk, run, and skip around the room while repeating the word for the action simultaneously.

Settling Time

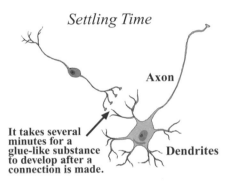

Settling Time

Axon

Dendrites

It takes several minutes for a glue-like substance to develop after a connection is made.

The design of the human brain is such that it cannot continuously learn an unlimited amount of new content. Most educators feel pressured to "cover more material" in the time allotted. This is a serious mistake. You can pour all the water you want into a glass, but eventually it will spill over. I'm not suggesting that our memory capacity is small, like a cup, but indeed, the stop-over station for processing the information before it's stored in long-term memory is small. The hippocampus, a small crescent-shaped structure in the temporal lobe, learns fast, but has a small memory capacity. Yet this is the mechanism that organizes, sorts, and processes the incoming explicit information before it is routed to various areas of the cortex for long-term memory. Thus, as teachers, we need to slow down and give students the time for new learning to settle.

Too Much, Too Fast, Won't Last

The design of the hippocampus is more suited to a short burst of information followed by processing the information, followed by memory formation, and then some down or "settling time." There is some evidence that time spent *not learning* new content is very important (Pellegrini, et al. 1995). In addition, the immature nervous system and huge amount of pruning that is happening up to age sixteen tells us that, if anything, we need to give more breaks than we currently do, not less. Psychology professor David Bjorklund says, "Young children in particular may require more breaks from seatwork" (Bjorklund and Brown 1998).

But adolescents and adults also need breaks away from content, too. As a good rule of thumb, if your learners have high background in the subject (in other words, the material is familiar), content acquisition can effectively last up to twenty minutes uninterrupted. However, if your learners' subject background is low, content acquisition may only effectively last up to twelve minutes uninterrupted. Then following the acquisition period, should be a period of settling. Remember your goal is not to "cover" the material, but for your students to learn it. Use this sequence: 1) Prepare learners with prior knowledge before the new content is introduced; 2) Make the acquisition stage non-threatening and deliver content at a comfortable pace; 3) Give learners time to process the new material, personalize it, and get feedback on it; 4) Provide settling time for the new content to get embedded in long-term memory.

Meaning-Making Is State Dependent

Everyone wants students to make meaning out of what they learn, but meaning is generated from within the learner. And the number one influence on what kind of meaning is made is—you guessed it—one's mood or "mind-body state." When you give out an assignment and students groan, this is partly the teacher's fault. Why? Because as the teacher, we need to better manage our learners' mind-body states. Did you make an effort to create an ambiance of curiosity and challenge before presenting the assignment? Have you made efforts to better empower learners so that they learn to manage their own states? If you give directions for a task and get a response of groans or student resistance, this is a teacher problem. Think about it from the student point of view. If I'm a student, and I'm distressed or depressed, whatever the assignment is, I'm going to complain. But if I'm in an excited state, it's different. The state your audience is in will modulate the meaning they make. In a good state, they'll interpret what you say more favorably.

So, what do we do? We need to better manage student states and teach them how to better regulate their own states. As we do this, students learn over time to take more responsibility for how they feel and for changing their mood when necessary. You don't believe me? Let's test my "state-dependent meaning-making hypothesis." Ask students to sit back in a slumped posture and put a frown on their face; then give them the next assignment and wait for their response. It will be negative! Now reverse the trend with positive actions! Ask them to stand up, take a deep breath, give their neighbor a positive affirmation, then listen to your brief assignment while standing. You'll get the opposite effect! Remember, movement is the best manager of students' learning states. Have them affirm, "I believe in action and activity." The brain learns best and maintains maximum efficiency when the organism is actively involved in exploring physical sites and materials and asking questions to which it actually craves answers. On the other hand, passive experiences tend to attenuate and have little lasting impact (Gardner 1999).

Guidelines for Play

1. Keep the motivation intrinsic:

Avoid using rewards as part of the play process. Let learners get engaged in the activities to such a degree that they don't think about external gain. Studies suggest that greater learning is associated with activities that avoid rewards (Pintrich and Schunk 1996).

2. Orient learners towards the process, not the goal:

This increases the chance that students will take charge of their learning and sometimes even shift their goals. The value of this is obvious: You'll see greater creativity, self-efficacy, and extension of existing learning.

3. Use non-literal frames of reference:

It makes sense to allow children to take on new roles, try out new behaviors, and experience things they might never experience beyond playtime.

4. Keep the rules simple:

Make sure every student understands the ground rules before an activity is ever attempted, particularly the safety rules and what to do in an emergency. Be prepared to alter the rules, as necessary, for your particular group of learners.

5. Include everyone:

Use games that everyone can play, even if some adaptation is necessary. Games ought not be for the most fit, the most intelligent, or the best versed. Get everyone involved: Everyone can learn.

Indoor Movement Ideas

| **Use the Body to Learn** | Have learners stand up and demonstrate concepts like big or small, tall or short, quick or slow. They'll have more fun demonstrating words like crawl, roll, and feeling surprised. Have them form small groups and play counting games. Kids can form shapes of numbers with their bodies, touch elbows to elbows, feet to feet, etc. Explore textures through classroom scavenger hunts. Demonstrate left and right hands by raising and shaking them. Clapping or stomping out rhythms, words, or beats can make this activity more fun. If you think these activities are only for kids, you've lost the joy of learning and the point of this whole book. Adapt! |

| **Facilitate Creative Role-Plays** | Get your class used to daily or, at least, weekly role-plays. Have students do charades as a review of main ideas, or organize extemporaneous pantomimes to dramatize key points. Do one-minute commercials adapted from television to advertise upcoming content or to review past content. With adults facilitate a three-minute standing session whereby one learner gives a quick review of the learning to the other in a pair share. Make it more challenging by allowing gestures and movements to relate to the learning. Or have adults do a little skit as a group to emphasize key points, or make a commercial, or go for a walk and pair share. |

| **Incorporate Energizers** | Use games, activities, and energizers found in this book or in other books. For example, "body measures" is a great energizer. In this activity, you have learners measure items around the room with their body and report the results: "This cabinet is 99 knuckles long." Play Simon Says with content built in: "Simon says point to the South; Simon says point to five different sources of information in this room. Do team jigsaw processes with huge, poster-sized mind maps. Get up and touch seven different colors around the room in the order of the color spectrum. Teach a move-around system using memory cue words: "Stand in the room where we first learned about such and such...." |

| **Teach Goal-Setting on the Move** | Start class with an activity in which everyone pairs up. Students can charade or mime their goals to a guessing partner or go for a short walk while setting their personal goals. You might have them answer three focusing questions, such as (1) What are my goals for today and this year? (2) What do I need to do today and this week in class to reach my goals? And (3) Why is it important for me to reach my goals today? You can invent any questions you want or ask students to create their own. |

| **Play Review Games** | Ball toss games are great as a review for vocabulary-building, story-telling, and self-disclosure. Students can re-write lyrics to familiar songs in pairs or with a team integrating new words and concepts that represent learned content. Then they can sing the song or perform it with some choreography. Get physical. Play Tug-of-War or a "Verbal Tug" where opposing sides are debated with a partner. The goal, of course, is to convince the partner in a thirty second argument why a viewpoint is right or, at least, worth considering. After the verbal debate, the whole class can release pent up energy with a giant Tug-of-War game with partners on opposite sides. |

| **Facilitate Cross-Laterals** | Arm and leg cross-over activities are simple and easy to use. They are a powerful aid in that they force both brain's hemispheres to "talk" to each other. With your left hand, pat your right ear, shoulder, elbow, etc. (cross-laterals), or pat your head and rub your belly simultaneously (cross-overs). Cross-overs include marching in place while patting opposite knees, or patting yourself on the opposite shoulder while touching opposite elbows or heels. Several books, including *Brain Gym* by Paul and Gail Dennison (1989) and *Smart Moves* by Carla Hannaford (1995) describe these activities in detail. |

| **Incorporate Stretching Activities** | As a class opener, or anytime you want to get more oxygen flowing to the brain, get everyone up to do some slow stretching. Rotate students to lead the exercises. Overall, provide learners with more freedom of mobility in the classroom during specific times, as well. Make a jump rope available, allow learners to run an errand for you, or simply let students walk around the back of the room as long as they avoid disrupting other learners. |

| **Use Laughter** | Ask students to stand and practice a big group laugh. After you share something funny with the group, invite them to find three or four others with whom to form a "standing joke" circle. Once individuals within their groups have shared a joke or two, ask the small groups to contribute their best joke to the larger group. Finish with another big group laugh. There's evidence that a even a few moments of laughter is good for the body and mind (Dhyan 1995). |

Time for a Break!

Before enjoying this book any further, now is a good time to pause for a break. I would recommend that you do something active, like one of the following suggested activities, but NOT more reading. At least, not just yet.

✦ **Stand up and stretch for a minute.**

✦ **Go get a glass of water and rehydrate.**

✦ **Find a quick chore to do.**

✦ **Go for a five-minute walk.**

✦ **Put on music and dance.**

✦ **Reflect on your learning and take notes.**

✦ **Do some cross-lateral motions.**

After you've taken a brief break, then come back to the book. Remember, the power of learning means you have the capacity to change and integrate new information beginning immediately. So why not start a new habit right now. Let's embody the new learning before we try to effectively teach it to others. We learn the most through example, imitation, and role modeling.

Take the message of movement and begin applying it now. Remember, if you don't live it, you don't believe it.

CHAPTER FOUR

+ **What the Science Says**

+ **Creativity**

+ **Social Skills Enhancement**

+ **Motivation**

+ **Perceptual-Motor Enhancement**

+ **Self-Discipline**

+ **Cognition**

+ **Emotional Intelligence**

+ **Self-Esteem**

+ **Performance Suggestions You Can Use Today**

Performing Arts

An analysis of nationwide college entrance exam scores indicates that a potential correlation may exist between performing arts involvement and higher test scores. The College Board reports that students with just one year of performance training demonstrate higher scores and that those gains grow exponentially with the number of years of arts involvement. The national average for SAT scores, for example, is 1,015 (combined); however, students who are involved in jazz ensembles average between 30 and 200 points higher. While this relationship is not causal, a plausible explanation may be that the inherent benefits of performing arts involvement, such as discipline, focus, emotional expression, creativity, memorization, stress reduction, enjoyment, and friendships, when taken as a whole, make an important contribution to learning. This chapter explores that hypothesis.

As we examine the role of dance, drama, directing, choreography, kinesthetic awareness, improvisation, mime, musicals, and other like mediums, it is important not to assume that any haphazard addition of these activities to the curriculum will improve learning. We all know that any learning program must be accompanied by solid implementation strategies to be effective. Just throwing out a ball at P. E., so to speak, undermines the potential benefits of innovative teaching and learning practices. To maximize the benefits of a performing arts program, the program needs to be strategically planned with short- and long-term goals identified. The activities need to be challenging, safe, relevant, fun, and inclusive. While learners ought to be well versed in the rules, there should be no embarrassment, ridicule, or punishment for breaking them. And, ample feedback mechanisms should be built into the process.

What the Science Says

While a solid performing arts program offers many direct benefits, one indirect benefit is that, as a form of play, theatrical involvement facilitates the maturation of the brain's cortical systems (Allman 1999). Activities, for example, that include spinning and body rotation, such as dance steps and cartwheels, may be essential in the formation of critical brain areas responsible for controlling spatial, visual,  auditory, and motor functions (Palmer 1980). Movement activity, especially when it engages multiple brain systems, seems to accelerate learner maturation. Even the simplest games and energizers that involve turnaround activities and spinning can strengthen early brain function. And yet, they are usually underutilized in the classroom setting.

One study suggests that using gestures while speaking increases the likelihood of recalling words (Krauss 1998). Not only does our brain activate our motor movements, but the reverse happens, as well. Kicking your feet, for example, activates the part of your brain that corresponds to the initiation of that movement. There are many links between our brain and our body, and activating one can activate another. What this all means ultimately is that by moving our body (as in the performing arts) we can better access our brain.

Studies on enrichment indicate that certain conditions that enhance the growth of cell bodies, increase dendritic branching and add neural connections. While we know that learning also involves the natural pruning away process of excess synapses, performance-related enrichment may speed up the process. Reading, counting, speaking, and problem-solving are all maturation-correlated activities. A child can't read, in other words, until his or her brain is physically capable of the task. The brain, however, may mature faster and more efficiently when the following primary ingredients for brain growth are involved: challenge, novelty, feedback, coherence, and time. The performing arts provide these ingredients. Students often choose, albeit unconsciously, the games they play precisely because they provide them with what they need—an appropriate challenge level, feedback, novelty, etc. Consider, for example, how many of the forenamed learning needs are potentially met in the production of a musical.

Creativity

Play facilitates our creativity. Children who are played with learn to play. Metaphors and symbolism—important elements of creativity—are also developed during play. From Aesop's Fables to Grimm, from playing house to Ring-Around-the-Rosey, all of these stories and games provide mythical and real representations of the world. However, by age seven most students are ready for more objective, less dreamy symbolism. This is a great time to introduce dramatic play. Dramatic play provides a link from the inner world to the outer world and provides a stage for developing social skills.

The Value of Vestibular Stimulation

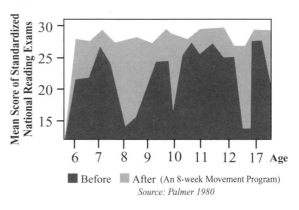

Mean Score of Standardized National Reading Exams

■ Before ■ After (An 8-week Movement Program)
Source: Palmer 1980

Performers have trained their brains to work a bit differently compared to the rest of us. Neurologist Marcus Raichle of Washington University in St. Louis says our brain's concentration centers are in the left-frontal lobe and in two areas of the right side of the brain (Posner and Raichle 1994). When the brain of an expert performer is viewed with an imaging device, we see a burst of alpha wave activity in the left side of the brain, the more analytical side, at the outset of a dramatic performance. During a peak performance, the left side of the brain relaxes and the right side takes over (Allman 1992). The result is the "flow" state that many performers report as the zone of optimal performance. Far from a right-brained frill, performance arts facilitate whole-brain skills like concentration and motivation.

Collectively, our current understanding of neurobiology suggests that we might want to incorporate more, not less, body movement and play into our curriculum. We have ignored implicit learning for far too long. In fact, noted neuroscientist and memory expert Dr. Arthur Reber (1993) says, "Unlike contemporary approaches to pedagogy and instruction, the results from the studies on implicit learning suggest that school curricula should be modified to include more exposure to the variations that the specific subject matter displays... a tilt towards the kinds of educational programs championed by John Dewey." This calls for more movement, more activity, and more reliance on implicit learning.

**Creative   Controlled
Student   Student**

Students in performing arts programs are encouraged to use creative thinking skills. Such training may help develop broader life skills, as well. One study examined the value of integrated learning through dance and music. The children (four- and five-year olds) were divided into four groups: (1) independent study, (2) verbal instructions, (3) verbal instructions plus acting out the related movements, and (4) instructions given in song with music and movements incorporated in the form of a dance. After twenty days of exposure to the experimental conditions, the Torrence Test of Creative Thinking was given to all subjects. Obtaining the highest scores was the music/dance combination group, while the other two experimental groups exhibited higher scores than the independent study/control group (Mohanty and Hejmandi 1992).

In another study, high-school students involved in theater outperformed non-theater students on a creativity test (Hamann, et. al 1991). A common skill that both theater and dance students are asked to perform is improvisation. This requirement may prime the brain for creative ideas. Rarely is creative behavior rewarded in a typical pencil and paper classroom. Can you imagine a student saying to their teacher, "Hey, I have a new theory of gravity" (or relativity, or motion)?

Social Skills Enhancement

We've long known that social skills are influenced by the interplay between multiple brain systems: the orbitofrontal lobes, our communication areas in the parietal and temporal lobes (Wernicke's and Broca's areas), our midbrain emotional systems including the thalamic and amygdaloid structures, and ultimately our chemical messenger system in the brain, called peptides. These systems need practice, practice, and more practice to mature and develop optimally.

Performing arts training is a powerful tool for developing these brain systems. It provides a stage for young people to relate with the opposite sex in a nonthreatening setting that includes social discipline and emphasis on courtesy and consideration for others. Working together towards a common goal creates synergy. The close contact of dramatic arts often requires balance, coordination, and synchronized movements. The process of interacting with others in a structured setting provides markers for acceptable social behavior.

Pantomime is an excellent tool for teaching social skills. The material is endless. Something as simple as, "Show me how you would react if someone was rude to you," or, "Show me how you would greet a best friend who just returned from a long trip," can produce a great deal of thinking, physical practice, and reflection. Pantomime allows for the development of nonverbal skills, social confidence, and combining thoughts and actions (McCaslin 1996). Very young children respond well to pantomime practice such as, "Show me a hungry lion." Later, children can perform more complex task performances such as, "Show me a clown that is making a group of children laugh." A similar approach is to play charades. To expedite this activity, create a custom deck of cards with a single idea (related to content preferably) listed on each card. Then have each student select a card from the pile to act out. The spontaneity and expression these activities inspire are healthy for emotional and social development, as well as for retention of new content.

The driving force behind a school drama or dance program is not to prepare students for careers in the performing arts. Rather, the expectation is to develop students' emotional, physical, and cognitive abilities through physical training. Some of the goals are to express personal ideas without fear or censorship, to discover the beauty of movement, imagination, and choreography, and to be introduced to compositional structure, sequencing, collaboration skills, and interpretation. The qualities of rhythm, coherence, and flow are also introduced and eventually refined. Technical skills such as artistic problem-solving, time-space issues, emotional impact, and production logistics are also inherent.

Motivation

An issue that plagues classroom teachers is learned helplessness. Some chronic failure in school can be attributed to this condition (Peterson, et. al 1993). In a nutshell, learned helplessness is a chronic and severe maladaptation to the environment. The most characteristic behaviors of learned helplessness are

(1) behavior inertia—inappropriate passivity with the glazed eyes look, often down and away from the teacher's desired focus of attention; (2) comments like, "Why try?" or "Who cares"? and (3) impaired academic achievement. Most teachers have experienced the frustration of working with students who have this condition. A chemical analysis of the brain of these students would show chronic depletions of the critical chemicals—acetylcholine, dopamine, GABA, norepinephrine, and serotonin. These neurotransmitters are the fuel for thinking, planning, feeling good, and taking action. So, can performing arts training positively impact this group of demotivated students? Absolutely, yes!

What the research tells us is this: While therapy can be a contributing factor in dealing with this disability, there's something much better. The most important thing is to "rewire" the brain, to create the mechanism that begins producing the chemicals necessary to cope. Nothing is more effective than feeling successful and rebalancing the chemical soupbowl through active movement.

If you have a student that is unresponsive, incorporate more physical activity. At home this means household chores, companion animal care, garden care, and involvement in active hobbies and recreational pursuits. Away from home it means participating in the scouts, doing volunteer work, or taking classes in which physical movement is required (i.e., gymnastics, martial arts, aerobics, etc.). Immersion programs such as Outward Bound, SuperCamp, or an expedition trip (i.e., river rafting, mountain climbing, cross-country skiing, etc.) are also excellent ways to help students with learned helplessness find empowerment. At school, get these kids involved in performing arts, athletics, and student activism. In the classroom, incorporate relays, dance, Simon Says games, stretching, physical games, drama, and music.

All of these activities force students to make significant choices, and they get the body moving. But one thing that stands out about the performing arts is that it offers high levels of social interaction, mental stimulation, and clear cause and effect while providing consistent feedback and support. In conjunction with a good performing arts program, students with learned helplessness need to be encouraged through a supportive healing process, such as journaling, learning logs, writing in a diary, and having the ear of a good adult listener. And this needs to happen over time; months are better than weeks.

Perceptual-Motor Enhancement

All of us, at one time or another, have mentally rehearsed for an upcoming task or performance. Mental rehearsals during practice and just before a performance reduce error rates. One study measured the ability of dancers to recreate music pacing in their head. The reproducibility of these mental performances was astonishingly accurate. While dancers and non-dancers equally estimated short intervals of 10 seconds (average error rate was 28%), dancers were more likely to accurately estimate longer intervals from 40 to 90 seconds (average error rate was only 1 percent or less) (Michon 1977). This suggests that the longer the time for mental rehearsals, the greater the alignment of cortical activity resulting in smaller temporal variability. Apparently dancing enhances our temporal-kinesthetic relationship, a valuable skill used daily for such time and space functions as driving.

Self-Discipline

The effort involved in producing a theatrical performance is significant. Typically, classes meet every other day, and, when rehearsing for a major performance, six days a week of practice is not uncommon. This places a huge load on the student. How does the typical performing arts student cope? Discipline! They are forced to become more efficient, just as an athlete is. From studying to listening to instructions, students learn to be more efficient when they have to. In fact, listening to directions is actually a series of tasks requiring the interplay between attentional systems, cognitive systems, short- and long-term memory systems, perceptual-motor systems, and visual and auditory systems. Dramatic arts can enhance all of these systems.

Cognition

The cognitive value of movement and theater in schools should not be underestimated. In a report funded by General Electric and the John D. and Catherine T. MacArthur Foundation, seven nationwide studies were analyzed. In one kindergarten class, kids danced their way through the prepositions with a rhythm background played by a Nigerian percussionist. In a fourth-grade class, kids created a huge playground map of the United States and literally ran from state to state, learning to identify them by movements. And in ten high schools where a Shakespeare program was presented, nearly eight-hundred students almost unanimously reported that they developed a strong sense of their own capacities through the program. Additionally, many said their success with Shakespeare carried over to other complex works of literature, and impacted math and physics, as well (Leroux and Grossman 1999).

In a Seattle, Washington, study, third-grade students learned language arts concepts through dance activities. Although the district-wide reading scores showed a decrease of 2 percent overall, the students involved in the dance activities showed a MAT reading score boost of 13 percent in six months (Gilbert

1977). In Aiken, South Carolina, Redcliffe Elementary's test scores were among the lowest 25 percent in the district. After a strong arts curriculum was introduced, however, the school's test scores soared to the top 5 percent in six years (as students progressed from first to sixth grade). This Title 1 rural school with a 42 percent minority student base showed that a strong arts curriculum is at the creative core of academic excellence—not more discipline, higher standards, or the three-Rs (Kearney 1996). "Now, kids truly look forward to coming to school," says Redcliffe's principal.

With a 100 percent minority inner-city population in the poorest congressional district in the United States, St. Augustine Catholic School (K-8th grade) provides a true testament to the value of a performing arts curriculum. In a district—South Bronx, New York—where other schools have a 25 percent graduation rate, this school stands out. By building its entire curriculum around the arts, this school's student engagement, motivation, problem solving, and creativity have soared. But what about academics? Proudly, 98 percent of its students read at (or above) grade level, and 98 percent meet (or exceed) the state's academics standards. If you're looking for miracles, look no further. These kinds of extracurricular activities are positively correlated with improved relationships, greater motivation, and academic improvement (Gerber 1996).

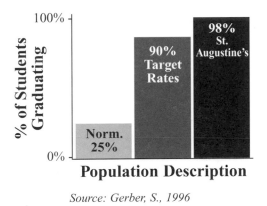

Graduation Rates of Bronx, NY School with/without Movement Arts

Source: Gerber, S., 1996

Emotional Intelligence

How important is the ability to feel when it comes to learning? It is much greater than you might think. It is not enough that we have multiple coping systems that tell us what to do to help us survive. Other systems must be at play, as well, to help guide us in our daily decisions. Nature could not have anticipated a world in which information would be doubling every sixteen to eighteen months, when only a century ago, it was doubling every 250 years. At this pace, multiple systems must be working in sync to thrive: The human emotional system is key.

Emotions have a critical regulatory quality to our lives that should not be dismissed. Fear occurs when our survival is threatened; guilt occurs when we fail to repay a favor; and sadness occurs when we lose a family member. Feelings and emotions play an ingenious role in regulating the content and circumstances of how we learn. It's not enough to *know*, we must *feel motivated to act on our knowledge*. Feelings facilitate cognition; they determine how we reason in the world; and they help us determine what is important.

The performing arts allow us the opportunity to act out our fears, grief, and aggression in a nonthreatening way. Through performance-oriented outlets, students release worries, tension, and stress; they meet emotional challenges and ultimately gain emotional competence over feelings that might otherwise overwhelm them. Practice on this level helps learners stretch their range of expression, which is healing and stress-reducing in itself. We can release our secrets, our worries, joys, and problems in a tension-to-release format that's good for our mental and physical health.

Dance, for example, integrates all of these elements without the need to speak. When we ask learners not to talk and not to move for long periods of time, we're asking them to resist their natural state. Schools that make sitting the exception, rather than the rule, are giving young learners what their brain needs for optimal learning. Martha Graham said, "There is a vitality, a life force, an energy, a quickening, that is translated through us into action; and because there is only one you in all time, this expression is unique. And if you block it, it will never exist through any other medium and will be lost." Dance, in fact, conditions us to better regulate stress and gain a sense of control over our self (Hanna 1995).

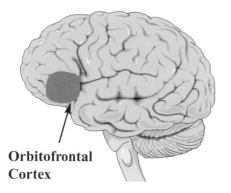

Where Our Brain Integrates Cognition, Sensation, and Emotion

Orbitofrontal Cortex

The areas of the brain most involved in managing our emotional responses include the orbitofrontal cortex (located right behind our eyes), the thalamus, the amygdala, and the reward pathway from the top of the brainstem through to the frontal lobes. "Emotional intelligence," the skill set that has been identified as one of the keys to success in the world, includes the ability to heal the devastation of earlier emotional trauma. Good emotional intelligence involves stress management capabilities and a healthy sense of self-esteem.

Humans don't learn in a random, haphazard way. Rather, learning is a highly selective and managed process with very specific rules for memory formation. The regulatory mechanism for this daily blizzard of complex decision-making and for our storage capability is not our logic, but our emotions. The countless decisions we must make every day are "weighted" by our emotional system, which analyzes information for meaningfulness. Learning is not a general-purpose mechanism that allows all environmental relationships to be acquired with equal proficiency. Instead it is a constrained mechanism that depends on an affective value system for providing immediate appraisal (Johnston 1999). We all have emotions; it's the ability to properly regulate the system that makes or breaks our overall intelligence. The emotions are key to it all. The movement and performing arts provide a valuable vehicle for exploring and expressing our human emotions.

In one study with one-hundred-plus subjects ranging in age from four to adult, expressive dance movements were taught and then decoding skills were measured (Boone and Cunningham 1998). While there was an expected range of skill levels, it was also discovered that decoding abilities (exceeding chance levels) were found even among four-year-olds. The dramatic arts practice seemed to encourage better emotional decoding. And, participation in the arts decreases the chance a student will drop out by 15 percent (McNeal 1995).

Self-Esteem

A common perception of both children and adolescents, and some adults even, is that the world happens to them. They believe that how they feel is generated by their circumstances, and as such, they lose their sense of personal control and responsibility. As a result, they experience a lessened sense of self-efficacy and empowerment, which often leads to depression. But students who participate in the movement and performing arts have more opportunities for control over their environment. They learn that they can even control how they feel. They learn that, for example, dance makes them feel good and that singing can raise their spirits.

Self-concept is simply the way we think of ourselves—our perceptions. But self-esteem is the value we hold of ourselves and how we feel about ourselves. Our self-esteem soars when we are good at something. Beyond the emotional expression dance provides, it also adds an element of physical conditioning. Students must master and coordinate many moves to gain proficiency. Commonly included in dance instruction is a healthy dose of support and feedback. In one study, dance was found to promote self-identity and social values (Hanna 1979).

One highly successful program used the following four-part plan to increase student learning through arts performance: (1) A process was developed to identify dance and musical talent; (2) Teachers began to notice positives about students that they had not previously noticed; (3) Parents were included in the process of identifying and nurturing talent; and (4) All participated in a disciplined effort towards the school-wide goal of increasing the students' learning and performance. Engaging ninety-six inner-city children, all third and fourth graders, the project lasted for three years and the positive results were maintained after the program's completion (Kay and Subontik 1994).

Performance Suggestions You Can Use Today

1. Nelson Neal, president of the National Dance Association, says that one of the most important concerns when incorporating dance into the curriculum is to make it fun without being embarrassing or threatening. One approach he uses is to ask a student to name a sport. Then he asks the class to name and describe the various moves and motions one would encounter while playing the sport. Then he models the motion and asks students to practice them with him on the dance floor in both slow and fast motion. Then he has them combine the moves from two or three sports and, ultimately, the group has choreographed a series of movements that kids enjoy.

2. Sue McGreevy-Nichols, a middle-school dance teacher, collaborates with the other teachers at her school to create dances that touch on academic issues appropriate to the students' grade level. In this way, dance and academics are integrated and are supported by the important elements of movement, discipline, reflection, challenge, and meaningfulness. This strategy also enhances the fun factor in learning for both the students and teachers.

3. Pantomime is underutilized in the school setting and is a highly effective tool for teaching appropriate behaviors. At the kindergarten through second-grade level, use simple actions with a command like "Brush your teeth" or "Tie your shoes" or "Eat an orange." At the third- through sixth-grade level, pantomime can be an effective tool for teaching social skills: "Show me how you would react if someone was rude you you." Or, "Show me how you would greet a best friend who just returned from a long trip." At the seventh through twelfth-grade level, pantomime is usually incorporated in the form of charades.

4. Finger plays and puppet plays are excellent for pre-K and kindergarten children. Avoid stage performances during these early years since the stage may actually inhibit the child's expression. Keep the plays simple and let children experiment with the process of playing, rather than performing. When children exhibit aggressive behavior, this is your cue to teach socially acceptable behaviors and model cooperation.

5. Story reenactment is also a good form of creative expression. Allow students to select either a well-known story (fables, poems, or favorite books) or to re-create a real event. This is particularly powerful for teaching social and moral behaviors. Have children reenact a classroom scuffle, a fight over possessions, or an occasion in which someone's feelings were hurt.

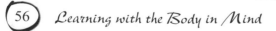

Time for a Break!

Before enjoying this book any further, now is a good time to pause for a break. I would recommend that you do something active, like one of the following suggested activities, but NOT more reading. At least, not just yet.

✦ **Stand up and stretch for a minute.**

✦ **Go get a glass of water and rehydrate.**

✦ **Find a quick chore to do.**

✦ **Go for a five-minute walk.**

✦ **Put on music and dance.**

✦ **Reflect on your learning and take notes.**

✦ **Do some cross-lateral motions.**

After you've taken a brief break, then come back to the book. Remember, the power of learning means you have the capacity to change and integrate new information beginning immediately. So why not start a new habit right now. Let's embody the new learning before we try to effectively teach it to others. We learn the most through example, imitation, and role modeling.

Take the message of movement and begin applying it now. Remember, if you don't live it, you don't believe it.

CHAPTER FIVE

Outdoor Play and Recess

Like other instructional activities, outdoor play and recess also require particular conditions to optimally enhance learning. Disorganized play, for example, may be fun for the kids and even valuable to some degree, but when courtesy, respect, rules, and high involvement are encouraged, the benefits soar. There should be well-defined goals and objectives for each activity, and games need to be appropriately challenging, safe, inclusive, relevant, and fun. It is extremely important that learners not be embarrassed, ridiculed, or rejected, so devise ways to form teams or groups when necessary that don't leave some learners feeling left out. Provide ample feedback throughout the process, and review goals and objectives with learners to reinforce learning and to evaluate the activity's effectiveness.

Daily recreational play ought to be included thirty to sixty minutes per day at the kindergarten through fifth-grade level. From middle school through university level, a fifteen- to thirty-minute period of "non-academic" activity for every three-hour block of content learning is sufficient. Suggestions for "down time" activities include going for a walk, taking a recess, offering water breaks, facilitating New Games, conducting outdoor relays, dancing, stretching, jump roping, role-plays, group play, aerobics, and simple sports activities.

What the Science Says

Researchers know that "play" plays an integral role in learning (Pellegrini 1984, 1995, 1998). While there are several theories about why humans play there is no disagreement that it is good for us. Although early cognitive researchers largely ignored play as a developmental process (assuming it was separate from developing the intellect), scientists now understand that the two processes are interdependent. Some of the types of play that schools ought to incorporate include the following:

- ✦ **Exercise play:** aerobics, running, tag, stretching, dance, pull ups
- ✦ **Functional play (skill oriented):** shooting baskets, hitting a ball, catching a Frisbee
- ✦ **Solitary play:** art, cards, object manipulation, crossword puzzles, mazes
- ✦ **Outdoor exploration:** digging, hiking, plant and insect identification
- ✦ **Team play (competitive):** relays, golf, tennis, Tug-of-War, flag football, kickball

- ◆ **Group play (noncompetitive):** New Games, earthball, dance, gymnastics, theater, chorus, band, drill team, cheerleading, Ring-Around-the-Rosy, London Bridge
- ◆ **Rough and tumble play:** soccer, football, wrestling
- ◆ **Constructive play:** building, Legos, blocks, model-building
- ◆ **Exploratory play:** Hide-n-Seek, scavenger hunts, make-believe
- ◆ **Individual play (competitive):** marbles, track and field, hopscotch, swimming
- ◆ **Adventure play (confidence-building):** ropes course, trust walks, outdoor camp, climbing, hiking, orienteering
- ◆ **Walking excursions:** to get a drink of water, to the cafeteria, media center, to run an errand, circle the building
- ◆ **Field trips:** theatrical performances, museums, historic landmarks, parks, aquariums

Proper brain function is dependent upon early motor development (Gabbard 1998). The period from two to six years old appears to be particularly critical to a child's motor development as muscle strength, coordination, balance, and spatial skills—which ultimately impact cognition—are initiated at this stage. The vestibular-cerebellar system (balance and coordination), also initiated at this time, orchestrates postural reflexes, eye movements, hearing, and other movements. Located in the center back of the brain near the thalamus with axonal projections to the visual system (occipital lobes), the somasensory cortex (parietal lobes), and the cerebellum, this system facilitates rapid and precise feedback regarding body movements to the brain.

Cognition and Movement Interplay

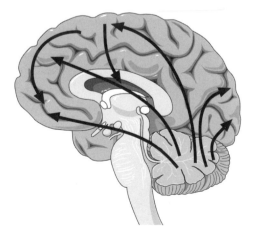

Each time you move your head, cupula (a gelatinous fluid) displacement causes movement in the cilia on hair cells which are embedded in your semicircular canals. These hair cells are similar to those found in your cochlea. The deflection of this fluid depolarizes the cell and allows the transmitters to be released, which activate the *outgoing* neural paths (axons). But this is a two way street. Nerve impulses from the brainstem (efferent pathways) that terminate on the hair fibers are *bringing* information to this part of the brain, as well. They have the capacity to alter the sensitivity of the hair cells while ideally providing precise regulation of movements (Barker and Barasi 1999). The cerebellum, in concert with the visual system, interprets the incoming information and responds by making the appropriate corrections in muscle movements. This delicate dance—input, feedback, and correction—is repeated in the brain all our waking hours.

The popularity of outdoor play seems to have diminished as our living standard has increased over the years. As we've become a nation used to comforts, being outside exposed to the elements has, perhaps, lost some of its appeal. When faced with the choice of going outside to play or staying indoors, many children consistently choose to stay in and watch TV or surf the Net. When balanced with outdoor exercise, movement activities, and play, there is nothing innately wrong with this choice. But, when the scales are tipped and children stop playing outdoors, important issues arise. Nationwide, students report greater disconnection from school; the physical fitness of our children is dropping; and health-related illnesses are up among children. How can outdoor play help? Let's start with social skills.

Developing Social Skills

The fact of the matter is that unless recess and playground play is organized in a purposeful manner and students are taught how to play cooperatively, the advantages of play can be undermined by the disadvantages. The other side of the coin, however, is that playground play offers the perfect opportunity to teach important skills, especially social skills, which ultimately impact a child's success in life.

Children can be aggressive and hurtful with one another. They must be *taught* appropriate behavior for resolving disputes and accepting differences. This "basic training" is often neglected in school recess programs. Increasingly, however, schools are beginning to implement strong positive social play programs. An example is Peaceful Playgrounds, which provides training for schools that are considering the cancellation of recess. Contrary to popular belief, recess is not a free lunch: Organizing playtime requires an investment in staff planning time and supervision. Adults need to take strong leadership roles on the playground to ensure that it works for everyone.

With sufficient structure and instruction, minor miracles can occur. In one study, researchers examined how physical activity influences moral reasoning (Gibbons, et. al 1995). The subjects were 452 students from fourth through sixth grades. Subjects were divided into three groups: (1) a control group, (2) a group with a "Fair Play for Kids" program intervention during the regular P. E. time, and (3) a group with a "Fair Play for Kids" program integrated across the curriculum. The seven-month experiment pre- and post-tested subjects with the Horrock's Prosocial Play Behavior Inventory (moral development indicator).

The positive results indicated that the children's moral reasoning skills improved significantly in the two experimental groups, but not the control group. Results were equally effective with both experimental approaches: Thus, it doesn't seem to matter whether the Fair Play program is instituted through physical education classes only or integrated across the curriculum. The study suggests that by training teachers and structuring fair play activities, positive changes in moral indexes occur.

Rough and tumble play may be more important to development in the social domain than earlier believed. Surprisingly, it may enhance emotional intelligence by facilitating the encoding and decoding of social signals. Two researchers who study this domain have said, "Despite the social consequences of such activity, the mechanisms involved are every bit as 'cognitive' as are those associated with math seatwork, thus expanding the realm of cognitive benefits afforded by physical play" (Bjorklund and Brown 1998). Further, they state that "some of the cognitive benefits of physical play are not 'incidental and serendipitous,' but a direct consequence of a specific type of physical play."

Researchers are also exploring a possible link between lack of infant stimulation and movement and violent tendencies later in life (Karr-Morse and Wiley 1997). Infants deprived of stimulation from touch and physical activity may not develop the movement-pleasure link in the brain. When fewer connections are made between the cerebellum and the brain's pleasure centers, a child may grow up unable to experience pleasure through usual channels of pleasurable activity. As a result, the need for intense states, one of which is violence, may develop.

Social and cultural differences are often obvious in children's play patterns, but keep in mind that differences are not deficits. In England, for example, children from lower socioeconomic backgrounds often exhibit more complex play behaviors (Tizard and Hughes 1976). Some children may demonstrate significant cognition skills in a play setting, and yet their capabilities may not be so obvious in the classroom (Griffing 1980). Cultural values are an important consideration when orchestrating play for youngsters: Activities have got to fit within the framework of the students' culture (Curry 1977). The presence of adults in some settings may change the quality and complexity of play, making it more constrained and simple (Pellegrini 1984), but it is, nevertheless, important to provide leadership on the playground so that children learn effective conflict-resolution skills. And keep in mind that differences between *how* children play are just that, not deficits.

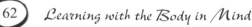

Play is a powerful and surprisingly efficient teaching and learning strategy.

Mind-Body State Changes

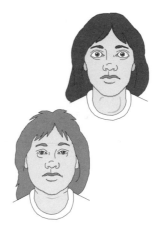

In any learning context, adults and children experience a wide range of mind-body states that impact attention, concentration, and recall. When negatively charged, it is a good idea to facilitate a change that might help the student move into a more positive frame of mind. Timing is important since the longer a student is in a negative learning state, the more bad associations they create with the environment, teachers, materials, and even the subject itself. Students who are in "stuck states" such as discouragement, confusion, or disappointment especially benefit from outdoor play. Since our behaviors are state-related, a change of state can eliminate undesirable behaviors.

Whenever possible, get students up out of their chairs, moving around, and learning outdoors, as well as indoors! There was a classic Peanuts comic strip in which Charlie Brown in typical fashion is standing with his head down, obviously depressed. When Peppermint Patty comes along and says, "Hold your head up high, Charlie, you'll feel better," he replies, "I want to feel depressed, so I'm keeping my head down." When educators make the connection between attitude and movement, they discover a powerful and efficient tool for adjusting learners' attitudes without focusing on the feeling.

Self-Esteem

A meta-analysis of the literature reveals that more than one-hundred studies link physical education and self-esteem. Of these, about one-third have sufficient quality of data (i.e., cross-sectional, quantitative, longitudinal, sequential or causal) to show that physical education significantly impacts how we feel about ourselves. Overall, 66 percent of all children in physical education (or directed play programs) exceeded the self-esteem scores of those not involved (Payne 1995). Physical fitness programs with clear objectives and good follow through were particularly singled out as beneficial to self-esteem.

Spinning Is Good for the Brain

Researchers know that certain movements stimulate the inner ear (vestibular system). Such movement subsequently impacts physical balance, motor coordination, and stabilization of images on the retina. With merry-go-rounds and swings disappearing from parks and playgrounds as fast as liability insurance costs escalate, there's a new cost incurred—more learning disabilities. Lyelle Palmer's studies (1980) suggest that certain spinning activities lead to alertness, attention, and reading skills in the classroom. Students who tip back on two legs of their chairs in class are often stimulating their brain with a rocking, vestibular-activating motion. While it's an unsafe activity, it happens to be good for the brain. One safe solution is to provide more opportunities for students to move around in school. Facilitate more role-plays, skits, and stretching sessions; and play more games like Musical Chairs, charades, and energizers. Best of all, it is painless and cost-free to incorporate more movement into your curriculum.

Stress Reduction

All of us are aware that some students consistently live with stress and even distress (excess levels) that accompanies them to school. When stress becomes chronic, cognitive problems can occur. Our hypothalamus, which is our brain's thermostat in many ways, initiates a series of reactions to deal with stress when it detects it. First a signal is sent to the adrenals, which release corticotropin releasing factor (CRF). The CRF then travels to the pituitary gland where it triggers the release of adrenocorticotropic hormone (ACTH). ACTH, in turn, stimulates the production of cortisol from the adrenals. Cortisol is good for a temporary energy surge, but at chronic levels, it inhibits adrenaline. So in the short run, stress is not harmful: In the long run, however, distress impairs learning.

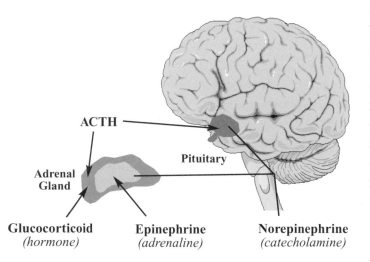

The Brain's Stress Response

ACTH

Pituitary

Adrenal Gland

Glucocorticoid *(hormone)*   **Epinephrine** *(adrenaline)*   **Norepinephrine** *(catecholamine)*

While a quick on/off stress response is healthy and helpful, long-term stress causes the protective hormones to shut off, weakening the immune system. As a result, the natural killer (NK) cells, which seek out threats to our health and destroy them, lose quantity and effectiveness. More prone to infection and disease now, our system is taxed. In school, this leads to more absences and less learning time. Chronic stress can also accelerate bone loss, impair spatial memory, weaken muscles, elevate blood pressure, impair short-term memory, destroy neurons in the hippocampus, and harden arteries.

A distinction can be made between energetic stress, such as the response commonly associated with the excitement generated by an athletic competition or physical challenge, and tension-stress, which activates chronically high levels of cortisol accompanied by dopamine or epinephrine release. While there is evidence that chronic tension-stress negatively impacts learning and memory, energetic stress likely aids learning.

Not surprisingly, movement plays a key role in the release and reduction of tension. In one three-week study, a group of college students were given three options during the day for responding to snack urges: (1) Go for a brisk walk; (2) Sit quietly and relax; or (3) Have a sugary snack. The subjects were instructed as to which option they were to use and when, and all were asked to carefully record their subsequent moods throughout the course of the experiment. The results indicated that walking was the best response for managing stress levels (Thayer 1996). Beyond the tension-reduction effect, going for a five-minute walk also reduced the subject's urge to snack and increased their energy, as opposed to a reported snack urge increase when subjects chose the sit and relax option.

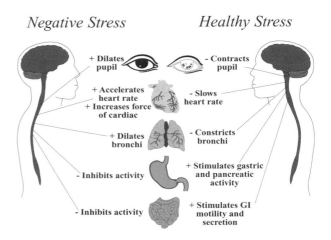

Negative Stress   *Healthy Stress*

When "Not Learning" Is Important

The Brain's High/Low Cycle

Some research suggests that one of the most significant benefits of recess is that it affords a break from cognitive tasks, thereby allowing new learning to settle (Pellegrini and Smith 1998). This down time is, in fact, essential to the learning process since the cortex absorbs and processes only so much new material at a time (Spitzer 1999). The hippocampus continually presents information to the cortex in micro bits, not truckloads. This micro stream of information, interspersed with pauses for processing (recess), prevents rapid widespread change that could threaten neural stability or survival (McClelland, et al. 1995). The organism is protected from overload by allowing only so much learning to be done before sleep or other down-time activities are required, relieving the brain of new input.

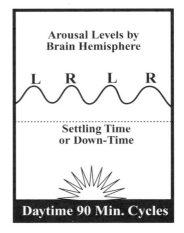

Down time is so elemental to our brain that it is built into our biology. Our brain completely shuts out new external input during sleep time and instead processes information previously obtained (Wilson and McNaughton 1994). "Young children in particular need more breaks from seatwork and more frequent changes in activities" (Bjorklund and Brown 1998). We simply cannot just "dump" information all day long into students' heads and assume they'll remember it.

Cognition

What happens in schools where frequent breaks from seatwork are instituted? Not surprisingly, academic achievement increases. Compared to the United States, for example, Japanese and Taiwanese schools are producing higher test scores in most disciplines, and yet first graders in Taipei (Taiwan) and Sendai (Japan) actually spend fewer hours in school than first graders in, say Minneapolis, Minnesota (Stevenson and Lee 1990). But the instructional approaches generally used in Japan and Taiwan are more brain-based. Although their instruction is more intensive, twice as many recesses are given and shorter school days are maintained for the youngest children. It makes perfect sense: Alternating periods of cognitive intensity and mental relaxation encourage efficient cortical maturation.

In spite of this, there are actually schools districts in America that have eliminated recess because they're afraid it's a waste of valuable, test-review time. But they are dead wrong. Any temporary gains in test scores that might possibly result from longer periods of instructional input will sacrifice the larger long-term goals of education. "Settling" time allows for the strengthening of synaptic connections in the brain that solidify prior learning. In this case, more is not necessarily better, and less is often more. For some learners, the social time inherent in recess may lower stress levels; while for others, the movement revs up their brain.

Here are some suggestions for maximizing the potential cognitive benefits of recess:

1. Get Active!

Incorporate some type of aerobic conditioning. This means reduce the standing around time at recess or P.E. Get learners walking fast, running, or playing games at a high energy levels.

2. Provide Sufficient Time!

Recess breaks should be at least thirty minutes long and up to forty minutes to maximize cognitive effects, say researchers Gabbard and Barton (1979). Alternate highly physical activities with less taxing ones and vary the challenge level. Too short of a recess can arouse students to a "hyper" state, which is counterproductive to learning. Too long of a break can tire learners and reduce their energy, rather than increase it. Thus, structuring break times appropriately is very important.

3. Consider Timing!

Breaks instituted at mid-day and early afternoon provide a greater benefit to students than an early morning recess (McNaughten and Gabbard 1993). Since a longer break is more productive than a couple of shorter ones, some schools make the mid-day break a lunch break, as well.

When Recess Isn't Working

More and more teachers and administrators complain that recess is simply not worth the trouble. They complain that students at recess are either out of control, or inactive, and that bullying is a common problem. These concerns are legitimate, but preventable. Recess problems begin in the classroom: Resolving them starts there too. Three of the root causes of recess problems include the following:

- **Lack of integrated classroom movement**
- **Poor emotional intelligence skills**
- **Serious emotional/social/toxic disorders**

The first problem is easily remedied: Provide students with more opportunities for movement and personal expression in the classroom. The more children are able to release their high levels of physical energy during class, the less likely they will go crazy at recess. Sitting for periods of more than ten minutes at a time is asking a lot of a third grader or a tenth grader. Games, energizers, and encouraging mobility will immediately reduce some of the problems we face at recess.

The second problem is a little more complex, but still remediable. Students need to have the values, expectations, and skills of inclusion, conflict resolution, sharing, and cooperation reinforced inside the classroom. While it's never a bad idea to include it outside, it's harder to manage the variables. The more social skills are emphasized in the classroom, the fewer problems you'll have on the playground. Most importantly, teachers must model these skills, as well as teach them. The performing arts, values-based games, and simple activities such as role-plays, provide a powerful forum for exploring the impact of our behaviors on others.

The third problem is largely out of our control. Many students come to school with serious disorders including anti-social disorders, malnutrition, traumatic stress syndrome, cognitive deficits, autism, fetal alcohol syndrome, and depression. Such disorders require specialized attention. A professional diagnosis is the first step, but often this is not a simple process. It is not uncommon for children to be misdiagnosed by multiple professionals. Once an accurate diagnosis is pinpointed, then questions often arise regarding appropriate treatment. While some troubled students can be helped at the classroom level, children with serious chronic disorders often need a much more structured and controlled environment than a typical recess program can provide. When you suspect a child may have a serious disorder, be sure to seek specialized help for them: They *need you* to go to bat for them! Don't kill a recess program because some learners need professional help. Keep the recess program intact for the majority of learners who, with appropriate structure, can greatly benefit from outside play!

Healthy Participation

One of the great benefits of play is the opportunity for inclusive participation. When actively involved in a team activity, learners feel important, they discover the camaraderie of low-stakes competition, and they learn about teamwork and cooperation. For this reason alone, every student from pre-K through college ought to be required to participate in some kind of physical activity. It is important to focus especially on those learners who may be left out of the loop. Traditionally, girls, noncompetitive boys, and learners with disabilities are allowed to flounder, when these are the very students who can probably benefit most from participation.

According to former Surgeon General Dr. Joycelyn Elders, girls who get involved in school sports are 92 percent less likely to use drugs; they are 80 percent less likely to have an unwanted pregnancy; and their high-school graduation rate is triple that of nonathletes. The importance of school sports is underscored when you consider the fact that girls who do not participate by age ten, have only a 10 percent chance of actively participating in a sport by age twenty-five (Elders 1994).

Get Outside

Today's learners increasingly spend ever greater amounts of time indoors. In Minneapolis, Minnesota, the average time spent outdoors annually was a paltry half-hour per day! In the more stable climate of San Diego, average time spent outdoors is double that of Minneapolis, but an hour a day is still too little. Lack of outdoor light can lower student learning and productivity. In 1973, as a response to the OPEC oil embargo, the United States government offices reduced the lighting in the Baltimore office from 1100 lux (one lux = 1 candle at one foot) down to 550 lux and to 325 in some spaces. Not only were many cases of eye strain noted (bad for reading and accuracy), but productivity dropped by 30 percent! A subsequent study noted that for every dollar saved on lighting, $160 was lost in productivity (Weiner and Brown 1993). That's a 160-fold loss!

Learners get too little bright light these days. School times increasingly translate to more time in darker environments. Lifestyle and safety concerns mean fewer children walk to school. Budget constraints mean inadequate school lighting, and ignorance keeps us from fully utilizing natural light. Children rarely see the light of day for six continuous hours. But is this really a problem? It could be a big problem, says Dr. Jacob Liberman, author of *Light: Medicine of the Future* (1991).

Liberman points out that over the past one-hundred years, the amount of outdoor light we are generally exposed to has declined. Ultraviolet light, present only in the outdoors, activates the synthesis of vitamin

D which aids in the absorption of essential minerals, such as calcium (MacLaughlin, et al. 1982). David Benton and G. Roberts (Lancet 1988) report that insufficient mineral intake has been shown to be a contributing factor in nonverbal cognitive deficiency.

If you dare get out of your chair,
go outside and get more air.

Depression impacts an increasing number of school-age children: Presently, estimates are about 5 percent. But exposure to bright lights for extended periods of time reduces depression (Yamada, et al. 1995). In addition, the presence of bright light can stabilize the depressing effects of sleep deprivation, which is a common problem among teenagers (Neumeister, et al. 1996). Evidence also shows that hospital patients who are in a bright sunny room heal faster. This finding suggests the potential health value of sunlight. But beyond the health benefits of outdoor light, students in brightly lit rooms and those who sit close to windows also perform better academically, according to a report prepared by the Pacific Gas and Electric Company (Unpublished: 1999).

In a very large blind study that examined the impact of environmental factors on learning problems, Dr. D. B. Harmon reported that more than 50 percent of children developed academic or health deficiencies as a result of insufficient light at school (Harmon 1951). The study, which evaluated 160,000 schoolchildren, also reported that when lighting was improved, problems were reduced dramatically, as depicted by the chart at the right.

Lighting Improvement Results

Problem	% Reduction
visual difficulties	65
nutritional deficits	48
chronic infections	43
postural problems	26
chronic fatigue	56

Another more recent study conducted by the Heschong Mahone Consulting Group in Fair Oaks, California (Unpublished: 1999), studied 21,000 students from three districts in three states. After reviewing school facilities, architectural plans, aerial photographs, and maintenance plans, each classroom was assigned a code indicating the amount of light it received during particular times of the day and year. Controlling for all possible variables, the study found that students with the most daylight in their classrooms progressed 20 percent faster on math tests and 26 percent faster on reading tests than students with the least lighting.

The best idea is under the sun,

get outside and have more fun.

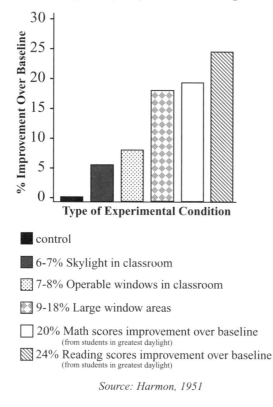

Impact of Light on Learning

Type of Experimental Condition

% Improvement Over Baseline

■ control

■ 6-7% Skylight in classroom

▨ 7-8% Operable windows in classroom

▨ 9-18% Large window areas

□ 20% Math scores improvement over baseline
(from students in greatest daylight)

▨ 24% Reading scores improvement over baseline
(from students in greatest daylight)

Source: Harmon, 1951

How can this happen? Light enters the eyes, travels through the visual system, the thalamus, and the suprachiasmatic nucleus (SCN)—our body's time clock, which helps regulate hormones such as melatonin and cortisol. Impacting important learning factors, such as sleepiness and stress, these hormones ultimately influence cognition. In addition, better light means better visual acuity and less eye strain. While bright light depresses these hormone levels, insufficient light sends a message to the brain that it's time to be drowsy or worried (cortisol is the hormone of negative expectations). Thus, some mood and learning problems can be minimized with exposure to more daylight and brighter indoor lights.

Sick Buildings, Sick Learners

Many learners are unknowingly exposed to health hazards daily at school. In fact, the typical classroom may pose significant environmental problems. All too common today in school buildings is the presence of building materials, products, and conditions that are toxic and hazardous to our health. A short list of some of these dangers follows:

✦ Adhesives
✦ Carpets
✦ Electronic fields
✦ Marking pens
✦ Paper goods
✦ Print cartridges
✦ Ventilation systems

✦ Allergies
✦ Cleaning products
✦ Formaldehyde
✦ Mold spores
✦ Nearby pesticides
✦ Radon
✦ VOCs (volatile organic compounds)

✦ Benzene
✦ Drapery chemicals
✦ Insulation
✦ Paint
✦ Pollen
✦ Synthetic fibers

Learning with the Body in Mind

These toxic by-products, even in small quantities, can cause serious learning problems over time. While some individuals are more sensitive than others to exposure, common symptoms include headaches, sneezing, dizziness, fatigue, nausea, and demotivation (Anderson 1991). The immediate solution is to get students outdoors more often. Long-term solutions, however, are usually more complicated and costly, such as installing better classroom ventilation systems. Surprisingly, students in *modern* classrooms come down with respiratory problems 45 percent more than those in *older* ones (Weiner and Brown 1993).

Motoring Up Motivation

The neural mechanisms that link exercise and motivation are probably very simple. First, if you already like exercise, then doing it may provide pleasure. Second, you may benefit from an increase in catecholamines (norepinephrine, dopamine, etc.), which typically serve to energize and elevate mood. Studies suggest that moderate running, however, does not produce excess or unusual adrenaline levels—the type that could disrupt classroom learning (Gillberg, et al. 1986). One major study of five-hundred Canadian schoolchildren reported that subjects who spent an extra hour each day in gym class performed notably better than less active children (Hannaford 1995).

Equipment Recommendations for Elementary-School Playgrounds

rope ladder
balance beam
tire or bucket swings
spring-based see-saw
hoops
ramps

slides
jungle gym
trampoline
horizontal (pull-up) bars
jump ropes
pogo sticks

Playful Ideas You Can Use Today

1. Triangle Tag

Divide the class into groups of four each. Three players form a triangle by holding hands; one of them is selected to be "it." The fourth player stands outside the group and tries to tag whoever is "it." The triangle team spins to protect the "it" from being tagged! The outside player and the "it" player switch places once the "it" is tagged and the role is then rotated.

2. Frisbee Review

Divide the class into groups of five or six students each and give them a Frisbee or ball or other object that is easily tossed around. Each time a player catches the object, they must share something they learned that day.

3. Walking Reviews

Pair and share as a means for reviewing past content. Have learners write up a list of questions and pick a partner. Partners go on a ten-minute walk and share their questions with each other (5 minutes each).

4. Body Machines

Role play how an assembly line or machine works: Pair up and act out a truck, computer, bar code reader, etc.

5. Triple Tag

A giant game of tag in which everybody is "it." Participants run around tagging other players. Once you've been tagged, you must hold that part of your body with one hand, but you're still in the game. The second time you're tagged, you must hold that part of your body with the other hand. The third time you're tagged, you're frozen in place. The last one still going wins the game. Footnote: The same person cannot tag you more than once.

Time for a Break!

Before enjoying this book any further, now is a good time to pause for a break. I would recommend that you do something active, like one of the following suggested activities, but NOT more reading. At least, not just yet.

✦ **Stand up and stretch for a minute.**

✦ **Go get a glass of water and rehydrate.**

✦ **Find a quick chore to do.**

✦ **Go for a five-minute walk.**

✦ **Put on music and dance.**

✦ **Reflect on your learning and take notes.**

✦ **Do some cross-lateral motions.**

After you've taken a brief break, then come back to the book. Remember, the power of learning means you have the capacity to change and integrate new information beginning immediately. So why not start a new habit right now. Let's embody the new learning before we try to effectively teach it to others. We learn the most through example, imitation, and role modeling.

Take the message of movement and begin applying it now. Remember, if you don't live it, you don't believe it.

CHAPTER SIX

+ *What the Science Says*

+ *New Cells, Better Brain*

+ *Self-Esteem*

+ *More Efficient Learning*

+ *Stress and Aggression*

+ *Grades and Test Scores*

+ *Perceptual-Motor Skills*

+ *Healthy Heart, Healthy Body*

+ *Motivation*

+ *Improved Discipline*

+ *Practical Exercises You Can Use Today*

Exercise and Fitness

At a major neuroscience symposium in Chicago where experts in the field of movement and cognition met, the message was clear: Our body enriches our mind. When a well-planned exercise program is followed, the brain is strengthened alongside the body. This chapter explores the role of running, swimming, jogging, weight training, fast walking, treadmill straining, and other aerobic activities in the teaching and learning process.

What the Science Says

Exercise Improves Mind/Body System

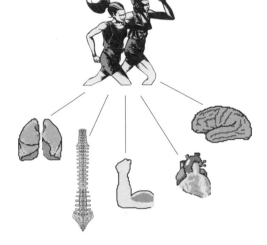

Physical exercise helps shape muscle fibers relied upon for adolescent and adult activities (Pellegrini and Smith 1998a). Writing, drawing, reading, and other detail work, for example, requires fine-motor coordination, which is developed through physical activities. Students who are engaged in daily physical education programs consistently show not only superior motor fitness, but better academic performance and attitude towards school as compared to their counterparts who do not participate daily (Pollatschek and O'Hagen 1989). Exercise increases the connections in the basal ganglia, cerebellum, and corpus callosum and enlarges capillaries around the neurons increasing blood to the brain. Exercise also fine tunes our attentional system while strengthening gross-motor muscles and our stress response. Beyond these benefits, a good exercise routine also boosts endurance, resilience, self-discipline, and motivation—factors essential to mastery of any skill or subject matter.

A survey of the studies on exercise and cognition show that while a mild walking program provides some health benefits, there's more to it than this. To maximize the benefits the exercise load should be adapted to the physical fitness of the individual. When subjects exercised until early exhaustion, cognition increases were more reliable. Short duration exercise, on the other hand, had minimal affect on cognition (Sparrow and Wright 1993). And, timing, memory, and decision-making tasks are negatively sensitive only to high physical strain with heavy exhaustion or apoxia (Fery, et al. 1997). Taken as a whole, this

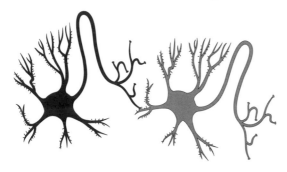

Neurons Connecting

suggests that a well-planned daily moderate exercise program can provide significant upside gain for learners with little downside risk.

New Cells, Better Brain

Over the last two decades, many studies have shown that exercise can lead to a better brain. While we've known for awhile that exercise increases synaptic efficiency, University of Illinois neuroscientist William Greenough and colleagues, in one of the most reliable and robust findings, demonstrated that exercising rats (on a treadmill) developed more connections between neurons (synapses) and actual nerve cell connectors themselves (dendrites) than non-exercising rats (Black, et al. 1990).

But the ultimate jackpot may be new cell growth. Neurogenesis was first reported in rat brains in 1965 by Joseph Altman, but few scientists believed the data. It took more than thirty years to confirm the finding in humans (Ericksson, et al. 1998; Kempermann and Gage 1999). While there are many similarities between rat and human brains, there are other issues that are being considered. Running, for example, may be the norm for rats in the wild, so the "increased" neuronal production subsequent to exercise may be unique to the species. The question thus follows: What's normal for humans? And a reasonable answer is, probably at least some rigorous daily physical exercise.

Subsequent studies confirmed that the new neurons quickly became functional in the hippocampus of the mice (Markais and Gage 1999). Although the new cell growth is only about one half of one percent of the total in the dentate gyrus, the running rats performed better on rat intelligence tests (mazes), completing them 20 percent faster than the control group (van Praag, et al. 1999).

Neurogenesis in Hippocampus

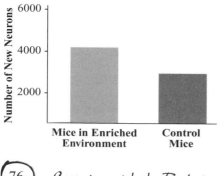

Although we now know that an enriched environment increases neurogenesis, we still aren't sure what the precise cause is. Enrichment conditions typically consist of expanded housing, increased social interaction, and greater learning opportunities. Gage and others are still trying to tease out which variables lead to the most substantial cell birth and neuronal preservation.

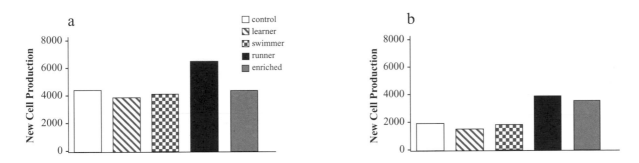

One Day Initial Neurogenesis   *Four Weeks Sustained Neurogenesis*

To test the variables, Gage's lab studied five groups of mice: (1) a control group in a standard setting with four mice to a cage and no exercise opportunities, (2) an enriched group with access to running wheels and toys, (3) runners encouraged to run about a mile a day on mice wheels, (4) involuntary exercise as swimmers, and (5) involuntary swimming lessons in a water maze. Of the five groups, two of them—the voluntary exercisers—exhibited astonishing growth of new cells in the hippocampus, the brain's learning and memory center (Kempermann, et al. 1998). While all of the rats grew some new brain cells, the voluntary runners grew more than twice the number as the "couch potatoes."

Some suspect that running produces not only more oxygen, but other vital nutrients such as growth factors, which promote neurogenesis. Another theory is that the very act of running may prompt the nervous system to prepare for an avalanche of new incoming information. Maybe the body responds to danger, a primary evolutionary motivation for running, by creating new neurons in anticipation of new learning. Neuroscientist Neil Cohen says, "Exercise over the eons may have become associated with a bunch of effects that help the brain prepare itself for new information, new learning, new brain work" (Hotz 1999).

Neuroscientists at the University of California, Irvine recently discovered that exercise triggers the release of brain-derived neurotrophic factor (BDNF)—a natural substance that enhances cognition by boosting the ability of neurons to communicate with each other (Kesslak, et al. 1998). A fibroblast growth factor is released with accompanying mRNAs and glial cells, leading researchers to believe that running may go straight to the core of learning—by producing chemical changes in the hippocampus (Gomez-Pinilla, et al. 1997).

The neurogenesis effect may also be related to the specific brainwave pattern—theta rhythm—produced in the hippocampus during physical exertion. Earlier studies have shown that a sort of "start signal" is triggered by locomotions such as running, which then stimulates the release of neurotransmitters such as acetylcholine and serotonin—the antidepressant neurotransmitters. Since depressed people exhibit some shrinkage in the hippocampus, there's some speculation that depression may impair neurogenesis.

Prior to this finding, one of the so-called immutable laws of brain science was that the human brain does *not* grow new cells. Dr. Fred Gage and his team from the Salk Institute of Neuroscience in La Jolla, California, and others, including Elizabeth Gould's group at Princeton, have sense shattered this long-standing belief. New brain cell growth may, in fact, be exercise's ultimate payoff.

If exercise encourages new brain cell growth, then shouldn't we also see better academic performances? The quantity of potential variables make an empirical answer to this question difficult. We look at studies by Terrence Dwyer and colleagues, however, for some insight. Pre- and post-tests were administered to measure three areas of performance: (1) fitness, (2) classroom behavior, and (3) academic achievement. In the first study, 519 children took part in what was called the SHAPE program. Over the course of fourteen weeks, the experimental group got four times the amount of exercise per week (375 minutes vs. 90 minutes) than the control group received. Although the experimental group's classroom time was reduced, their academic scores remained stable and their social skills and fitness improved. In the second study, the experimental group showed an improvement in both classroom behavior and academics (Dwyer, et al. 1996).

Overall, these findings suggest that voluntary running results in neurogenesis, improved spatial task performance, and an increase in long-term potentiation (LTP) in the hippocampus, believed to be important to learning and memory. The exciting news that humans can and do grow new brain cells daily, and that their production is enhanced with exercise, may possibly be as good as it gets! A strong fitness program may be more than good for the body; it's downright smart.

Self-Esteem

The most probable explanation for exercise's effect on self-esteem or social concept is that the "feel-good" chemicals, like dopamine and serotonin, are released in response to exercise, which indirectly influence self-efficacy. Repetitive gross-motor movements, like walking, swimming, and running, increase dopamine production, one of the brain's reward chemicals, and modulate our serotonin levels, a mood stabilizer. The secondary effects occur when one gains more control and, ultimately, mastery over one's body. Students feel good when they have control over their lives.

Students who are normally considered at-risk for low self-esteem are particularly helped by physical activity therapy. This group includes learners from lower socioeconomic backgrounds and those with learning disabilities, emotional problems, and/or physical impairments.

More Efficient Learning

Due to its thoroughness, large subject population, and longitudinal data, one recent study in particular is important to note. Although criticized for under-representation of minorities (only 10-19% of total), other studies demonstrate that physical education is equally valuable for minority populations. Standardized testing results using the MAT6 and MAT7 (Metropolitan Achievement Tests) were collected from district offices and coordinated with small-group data to determine the effects of a health-related physical education program on academic achievement (Sallis, et al. 1999).

The study included seven elementary schools in an affluent Southern California suburb with about one thousand student subjects. Three conditions were set up: (1) A certified physical-education specialist implemented a special program called SPARKS; (2) A trained SPARKS teacher implemented the same program; and (3) A control group was formed where kids participated in the regular physical education program, but not SPARKS. Students were pretested for physical fitness, social variables, and academic standing. The SPARKS program (Sports, Play, and Active Recreation for Kids) was rigorous with strong student involvement in all areas of activity. The program included goal-setting, coaching, and rewards.

Overall, the data supported the position that physical education programs are helpful, but don't necessarily boost academic scores—a tricky variable to manage. In this case, for example, the academic baseline was much higher than the national average, making gains potentially more difficult. Although this study demonstrated no significant gains on standardized tests, the authors discovered that the worse off the students were academically, the more likely they were to experience positive effects from physical education (ibid.).

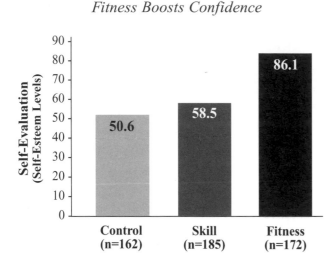

Fitness Boosts Confidence

Self-Evaluation (Self-Esteem Levels)

Control (n=162): 50.6
Skill (n=185): 58.5
Fitness (n=172): 86.1

The study concluded that the SPARKS trained teachers and specialists tended to spend more time on physical education than their non-SPARKS counterparts, but more time being physically active did *not* reduce academic achievement. So although less time was spent on academics, their scores remained strong. This suggests that perhaps exercise supports learning efficiency. And providing more movement education for teachers may have a positive effect on academic achievement. It is speculated that teachers may have experienced more relationship, authority, and integration value with the inclusion of physical activities in the curriculum. This, however, needs to be further investigated.

Stress and Aggression

"Children engaged in daily physical education show superior motor fitness, academic performance, and attitude toward school as compared to their counterparts who do not participate in daily physical education," say researchers James Pollatschek and Frank O'Hagen (1989). And University of Nebraska researcher Richard Dienstbier says that aerobic and other forms of "toughening exercises" can have lasting mental benefits (1989). The secret, he says, is that physical exercise seems "to train a quick adrenaline-noradrenaline response and rapid recovery." In other words, by working out our body, we better train our brain to respond quickly to challenges. Moderate amounts of exercise—three times a week for twenty minutes a day, for example—can have very beneficial effects, he adds.

Researchers know that chronic stress releases chemicals that kill neurons in the hippocampus, an area of the brain critical to long-term memory formation and learning. While athletic competition may increase aggression temporarily, noncompetitive exercise seems to inhibit it. This effect has been verified in both animal and human studies (Nouri and Beer 1989; Tanaka 1999; Widmeyer and McGuire 1997). In prison studies, weightlifting reduced aggression while team sports, such as football, increased aggression (Wagner 1997). With adolescent boys in a long-term care facility, the same pattern was found to be true (Mosseri 1998). These studies suggest that student behavioral problems may be reduced when more noncompetitive, nonaggressive physical activities are introduced into the school curriculum.

Grades and Test Scores

From movies and comics to ads and news shows, the athletic stereotype of the beer-drinking, class-dodging Cro-Magnon who can hardly cope without sports is imbedded in our culture. Outside of the physical education arena, athletes, dancers, actors, and other artists are generally perceived as noncacademics who inherited physical gifts at the expense of mental muscle. But advocates of physical education are standing up to this unfair stereotype. More and better studies are revealing the link between physical exercise and life success. We're also learning more about how best to teach physical education.

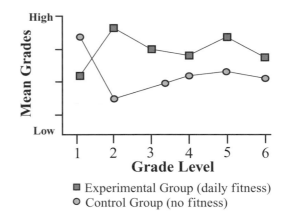

Fitness Group Maintained Higher Grades

■ Experimental Group (daily fitness)
○ Control Group (no fitness)

Obviously, there are many students in athletic programs who are not Rhode Scholar candidates or on the Dean's List. Many of these students are not going to become intellectual leaders or vie for the next Nobel Prize. But you could say that about almost any population. Having said that, however, one can still make a strong case for school life success predictability of athletes versus nonathletes.

Taken as a whole, students involved in sports have higher grades and higher SAT scores than those who don't participate in sports. In Texas, for example, high-school athletes scored 17 percent higher than nonathletes on the ninth grade state-wide TAAS in 1990. While it's true that some athletes barely pass, these students are the exception. Nevertheless, they fuel the negative stereotypes about athletes. When we stop to consider how many nonathletes also perform poorly in school, however, it is easy to see how mistaken this stereotype is.

One study of 124 adult subjects demonstrated significant improvement in executive function tasks after undergoing an aerobic walking program as compared to a anaerobic stretching and toning program (Kramer 1999). Although stretching programs provide other benefits, such as stress reduction, it is interesting to note that it did not provide the cognitive enhancement effect that aerobic activity did. Another study supports the aerobic claim. Among three test groups, the one participating in vigorous aerobic exercise exhibited the greatest gains in short-term memory, reaction time, and creativity (Michaud and Wild 1991).

In Quebec, a one year study of 546 primary school children was done to determine the effects of a one-hour per day physical education intervention (Shephard 1996). The students were extensively pre- and post-tested in five areas: (1) speaking, writing, and listening; (2) foreign language (English); (3) natural science; (4) math; and (5) overall academic performance. The students in the control group received the same academic environment, but had approximately 14 percent more time devoted to academics than the experimental group.

The results were positive. The experimental group significantly outperformed the control group at grades 2, 3, 5, and 6. The study's author, however, cautions that, "Daily programs of physical education should not be introduced with the expectation that they will lead to major gains in academic performance." In addition, he emphasized that physical education may not contribute to huge gains, but that it seems to optimize academic time on task, while also providing important nonacademic benefits.

The President's Council on Fitness and Sports sums up the findings this way: All kindergarten through twelfth-grade students need thirty minutes a day of physical movement to stimulate the brain.

Running Makes Rats Smarter

1) More efficient rats take fewer steps

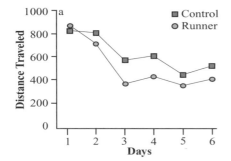

2) Sharper rats reach goal faster

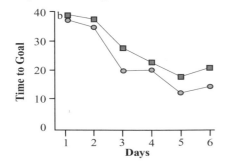

Perceptual-Motor Skills

Athletes learn to make rapid assessments under stressful conditions with a wide range of variables. Raw athletic ability never ensures success in sports. Beyond their physical prowess, the best players rely on their problem-solving and split-second decision-making abilities, timing, self-discipline, and risk management to succeed.

In basketball it's not the best shooter or passer who wins games, but the best decision-maker. With a tied score and five seconds left in the game, a player must decide to pass or shoot, keep driving, or throw up a prayer shot from half court. The decision involves calculating all of the variables in a split second—variables like the defense's weaknesses, teammates' strengths and positioning, and individual performance. All sports involve high level perceptual-motor skills, chance calculation or risk management, and ultimately skill execution (both body and mind).

Hockey great Wayne Gretsky was a talented skater, but so were many others. What set him apart was his ability to "think on his skates." He was a master at anticipating the moves of other players. In golf, what separates Tiger Woods from the other pros is not so much his technique as his thinking skills. Game strategy, club selection, and reading the environment are integral aspects of golf. Every sport requires a set of mental skills, and the cognitive decisions players make win or lose the game.

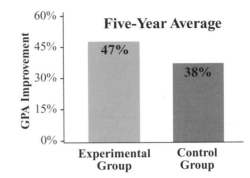

Athletic Mastery Improves Grades

Healthy Heart, Healthy Body

Physically fit people have better muscle strength, which leads to fewer accidents with less injury. A good fitness program also improves endurance, flexibility, and self-discipline. High quality physical education programs taught by a trained specialist play a significant role in the mental, emotional, and physical health of our children (Seefelt and Vogel 1986). Former United States Surgeon General Joycelyn Elders said, "Girls who participate in sports are 92 percent less likely to get involved with drugs; 80 percent less likely to have an unwanted pregnancy; and three times more likely to graduate from high school" (Elders 1994). And, "If a girl does not participate in sports by the time she is ten, there is a 90 percent chance that she will not participate at age 25."

Cellular Immunity

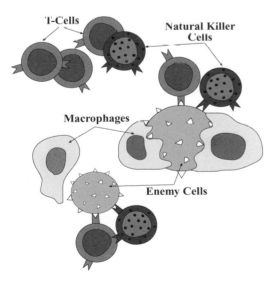

We have entered an era in which too many children do not participate in a physical education routine. Budget constraints have contributed to a convenient argument that the arts and physical education are merely "frills" that detract from academic success. This perception has become widespread in spite of the solid evidence to the contrary. When we stop making school interesting to students—dumbing down, rather than setting our sights ever higher—we alienate learners and discourage mastery.

In fact, research suggests that extracurricular activities are positively correlated with improved relationships, greater motivation, and academic improvement (Gerber 1996). Further more, there is evidence that grade point averages of both boys and girls actually increased while participating in sports programs (Silliker and Quirk 1997). Ralph McNeal

(1995) points out that participation in fine arts decreases the chances a student will drop out by 15 percent, and better yet, participation in school athletics decreases dropout probability by a whopping 40 percent!

Motivation

While many students complain that their physical education classes are boring, innovative educators everywhere across the country are learning how to change that perception. After all, why shouldn't physical education be exhilarating? That's the question Aldine School District in Houston, Texas, asked. The result is a district-wide wellness program for forty-eight schools that combines sports, fun, nutrition, exercise, academics, health, and safety. The foundation of this successful program is its commitment to relevant materials, full district support, additional teacher training, and a total, rather than narrow, approach to physical education.

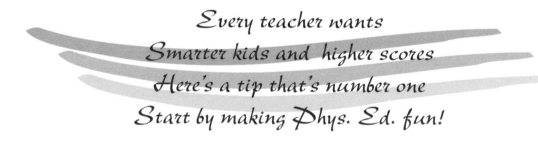

Every teacher wants
Smarter kids and higher scores
Here's a tip that's number one
Start by making Phys. Ed. fun!

In Vanves, France—a suburb of Paris—community leaders in the 1950s became concerned that school was too heavily weighted in book work and not active enough. A ten-year experiment was subsequently designed whereby a portion of the students were selected for a special program. This experimental group's school day was divided so that one-third of their time would be spent in physical education, while the other two-thirds were allocated for sedate learning. After ten years the two groups' affective and academic achievement scores were compared: Not only was the physical education group healthier and happier, but they exhibited fewer discipline problems and scored equally well, or better, in all academic areas (Martens 1982)

Improved Discipline

Is it really possible to reduce fights by increasing movement activities in schools? At Star Elementary school in Camden, Delaware, Pete Basile has instituted a walking program for kids as an alternative to recess. It's all by choice and someone records each lap they walk on a quarter mile track. In the 1999-2000 school year, students had walked collectively more than 19,000 miles! Students get healthy snacks like water, fruit, and nuts, and when milestones are reached, students get a t-shirt as a form of recognition. The year before the walking program was instituted more than one hundred playground referrals were administered. But with the walking program in place, they've had only two.

A solid physical conditioning program can enhance cognition, self-esteem, physical and mental health, perceptual-motor skills, and motivation, but maybe the biggest payoff is a sense of control over our lives. In a busy, chaotic, topsy-turvy world, contributing to students' sense of success and empowerment is vital to academic learning. Beyond providing learners with a valuable tool for managing stress, a good physical education program also, ultimately, supports greater satisfaction and peace in life. The gift of control and peace of mind, the gift that costs almost nothing and can be useful for a lifetime, is too important to dismiss as a "frill." It's time we take conditioning off the shelf labeled "For Athletes Only" and bring it back to the playground that asserts, exercise is a "Basic Human Need." We simply have too little to lose and too much to gain.

Practical Exercises You Can Use Today

1. Aerobic Dance
Incorporate Jazzercise, TaeBo, high-energy dancing, Jane Fonda Workouts, or any other aerobic routine that is fun and age-level appropriate. Start with very simple steps, and add a new one each day.

2. Power Walks
Running is not for everybody, but most people enjoy walking, and brisk walking provides many of the same benefits as running. Help students set time or distance goals to ensure they receive a good workout. Teach by modeling, as well. Make a habit of walking with a group of kids and get your movement needs met on the job.

3. Running

Early evidence suggests, thus far, that running may be the most productive exercise routine for growing new brain cells. While encouraging students to try running can be beneficial, forcing students to run can be counter-productive. Provide choices and create mechanisms to acknowledge and affirm learner progress. Students should be coached to wear a good pair of running shoes, to start with a realistic goal like running for twelve minutes, to record their progress, to drink plenty of water, and to continue to set goals for themselves. Tell students that if, after a week, they still don't like running, they can choose another aerobic routine instead.

4. Bicycling

Bicycling is a fabulous way to increase cardiovascular conditioning while exercising gross-motor skills and coordination. If rats could choose their means of exercise, perhaps bicycling would have proven more beneficial than running! Coach students to always wear a helmet, to pick safe and uncrowded areas to ride, and to follow all traffic and bike safety regulations. As with any aerobics routine, encourage learners to set goals and track their progress.

5. Swimming

Swimming is one of the safest and most beneficial exercises in the world. If you can access a pool, get students in the water! Although many children can swim well enough to stay afloat, the majority of them have never learned proper swimming technique—stroke efficiency, for example—that will support a thirty-minute aerobic workout. Coach students in water safety, lifesaving techniques, and physical conditioning workouts.

As always, to maximize the benefits of any exercise activity, it should be purposeful, challenging, fun, safe, inclusive, relevant, and structured so that all participants clearly understand the rules and objectives. Reduce the risk of learner embarrassment or rejection; supply ample feedback in the process; and devote at least one half hour per day, three days a week, to physical activity. Even a minimal exercise program, to start, can go a long way towards reversing the sedentary lifestyle that plagues much of our country today.

Time for a Break!

Before enjoying this book any further, now is a good time to pause for a break. I would recommend that you do something active, like one of the following suggested activities, but NOT more reading. At least, not just yet.

✦ **Stand up and stretch for a minute.**

✦ **Go get a glass of water and rehydrate.**

✦ **Find a quick chore to do.**

✦ **Go for a five-minute walk.**

✦ **Put on music and dance.**

✦ **Reflect on your learning and take notes.**

✦ **Do some cross-lateral motions.**

After you've taken a brief break, then come back to the book. Remember, the power of learning means you have the capacity to change and integrate new information beginning immediately. So why not start a new habit right now. Let's embody the new learning before we try to effectively teach it to others. We learn the most through example, imitation, and role modeling.

Take the message of movement and begin applying it now. Remember, if you don't live it, you don't believe it.

CHAPTER SEVEN

✦ **A Note to Policy Makers**

✦ **A Note to Staff Developers**

✦ **Where to Start**

Getting a Move On: Policy Implications

The Center for Disease Control and Prevention estimates that daily participation in school-based physical education classes has plummeted in the past few decades. The numbers tell the story: From the 1960s to the 1990s, student participation in physical education classes dropped from greater than 90 percent to less than 30 percent. Presently only one-third of kindergarten through twelfth-grade students in America participate in a daily physical education program (Simons-Morton, et al. 1999). This appalling number flies in the face of recent research that confirms the value of classroom movement activities and physical education programs, and it ignores the guidelines of The President's Council on Fitness and Sports, which recommends that all school-age children need a minimum of thirty minutes a day (at least 15 to 20 minutes at a time) of physical movement to stimulate the brain.

A Note to Policy Makers

Educators who are informed by the research now recognize that the most effective techniques for cultivating intelligence, social skills, and health, aim to unite (not divorce) mind and body. Both research and classroom practice clearly support sustaining (and increasing) the role of movement in learning. The positive cognitive, emotional, social, collaborative, and neurological effects are too strong to ignore. With the considerable potential for upside gain—physically, socially, and cognitively—it makes good academic sense to include a variety of movement activities

in every child's school day. In fact, from an ethical, scientific, and health standpoint, it is an imperative that all children be exposed to the movement arts on a daily, if not hourly, basis. As the effect of exercise and movement is especially great in the early years, a special mandate for early implementation should be enforced.

We have entered an era in which most children do not participate in a school physical education program. Every excuse in the book has been used: We don't have the teachers; we don't have the time; we need to get our test scores up; the weather is bad; it's too difficult to supervise so many high-energy kids; and the kids don't like it. Under closer scrutiny, every one of these reasons falls apart. The fact is that one-third of all schools do find a way to make it happen. Despite the fact that budget cuts often target the arts and physical education as "frills," the scientific evidence is to the contrary: The arts and physical education not only make school more interesting and meaningful to many students, they also help boost academic performance.

A Note to Staff Developers

You are the medium, the messenger, and the leader who can defend programs that support student success. Talking heads only reinforce the old stand-and-deliver approach, but the most revered staff developers model what they preach. Teachers look up to you. Administrators trust you. And, fellow consultants are proud to say they are on your team. While content mastery is important, we always learn more from what we *see* and *do*, rather than from what we *hear*. Today's students and teachers are depending on you to step up to the plate.

When you facilitate a workshop, offer fifteen-minute activity breaks every two hours. Build in compelling pair-shares; encourage meaningful exchange between participants; and plan activities that require teamwork, experimentation, and challenge. Telling participants to "talk to your neighbor" is *not* enough. Occasional group work is *not* enough. A one-hour lunch break is *not* enough. These activities hold limited kinesthetic potency. Raise the bar without raising the stakes. That is what this book is all about. Use the "65 All-Time Best Learning Activators" presented in the Quick Guide that follows; discover your own movement games; and ultimately, share your collection of activities with other educators.

Where to Start

As a staff developer myself, I have yet to conduct a workshop in which the physical activity level was sufficiently high. But compared to five years ago, or even a year ago, I've made a great deal of progress. It takes time, energy, and practice to incorporate physical movement every fifteen to thirty minutes. We didn't learn to do this in our teacher education programs, nor was it modeled for most of us in our own academic development. However, education practice has clearly evolved from an emphasis on straight content delivery to an emphasis on process—that is, grappling with concepts and ideas, discussing them with others, experimenting with models, testing theories, manipulating objects, and ultimately making informed decisions about the learning at hand.

At your next staff training, give participants the opportunity to feel more energy in their body and less chair on their derriere. Start the session with a stretching period. Play Simon Says. Ask participants to move to the opposite side of the room midsession. Give participants a walking assignment, even out of the building, if it's appropriate. Incorporate small group work. Facilitate experiments or mini-research projects. Reinforce content with a game of charades. Connect physical motions to new concepts or words to boost recall.

Give learners a sufficient challenge with which to grapple. Get them moving inside and outside the classroom. Role model active learning. Most of all, make a commitment to yourself that you'll never again be less than your best. Remember, your audience will remember what *happened* in your workshop far longer than what you *said*.

Move in, move up, move all around
Keep the brain and body sound
The more you move
The more you'll prove
That spinning and turning
Are good for learning.

Time for a Break!

Before enjoying this book any further, now is a good time to pause for a break. I would recommend that you do something active, like one of the following suggested activities, but NOT more reading. At least, not just yet.

- ✦ **Stand up and stretch for a minute.**
- ✦ **Go get a glass of water and rehydrate.**
- ✦ **Find a quick chore to do.**
- ✦ **Go for a five-minute walk.**
- ✦ **Put on music and dance.**
- ✦ **Reflect on your learning and take notes.**
- ✦ **Do some cross-lateral motions.**

After you've taken a brief break, then come back to the book. Remember, the power of learning means you have the capacity to change and integrate new information beginning immediately. So why not start a new habit right now. Let's embody the new learning before we try to effectively teach it to others. We learn the most through example, imitation, and role modeling.

Take the message of movement and begin applying it now. Remember, if you don't live it, you don't believe it.

QUICK
GUIDE

65 All-Time
Best
Learning
Activators

✦ **Best Indoor Games**

✦ **Best Outdoor Games**

✦ **Brainy Energizers**

✦ **Focusing the Brain**

65 All-Time Best Learning Activators

When incorporating energizers into your learning sessions, keep in mind that quick, simple, fun activities with a minimum of rules are best. Base your decisions on the group's needs; identify your intended purpose for the activity; and then implement it quickly so that you don't lose learning momentum. In this chapter, we provide you with sixty-five great activators that meet these criteria and are also able to serve a variety of purposes—from a quick state change or teamwork builder to enhancing memory or boosting energy. This list just taps the surface. You'll discover many others as you go along and ways to adapt them for specific groups or special purposes. Remember, it's most important to have fun!

Best Indoor Games

 **Body Machines**

Excellent means for bringing out creativity! With students working in pairs cooperatively, call out various types of machinery for the groups to act out—a car, truck, clock, computer, lawn mower, sprinkler, etc. Play music with a very definite beat in the background.

 **Instant Replay**

A great ice-breaker! With music playing in the background, have the group form a large circle or break into smaller groups of five or six students. Each member introduces him or herself by saying their name in conjunction with a gesture or body movement. The group imitates the motion. A variation is to go in order around the circle with each person initiating their own movement, then repeating, in order, the motion and name of each person before them.

 **Human Scavenger Hunt**

Wake up and take notice! The leader says something like, "Find and meet three others who..." and then adds a characteristic such as, like hiking, or are wearing your favorite color, or have the same initial as you. Repeat with variations.

Cheerleader Alphabet

Perfect for children learning their right from their left! Post a few lines of letters (about 3 lines, 5 letters each is good). Above each print an L (for left), R (for right), or B (for both). Then ask learners to name a letter. In conjunction with the appropriate hand-raising motion posted above the letter, the class repeats the letter and the motion. Variations on the game can make it more difficult.

 Contact

Good for a laugh! With background music playing, everyone stands, finds a partner, and follows the leader's finger-snapping, hand-clapping, or chanting rhythm. The leader then offers fun commands for making contact such as, back-to-back, foot-to-foot, hip-to-hip, or knee-to-knee, all initiated in conjunction with the rhythm. When the leader shouts "player-to-player"—the signal to change partners—the pairs reorganize. If the group is odd in number, a student rather than the teacher can lead.

 Clapping Games

Great for review! In small groups with music playing in the background, students stand in a circle and the leader starts a clapping or finger-snapping rhythm. Once the rhythm is established, each student offers something they learned in the course of the day. For example, "Today, I learned that California used to belong to Mexico." Then it's the next person's turn. That person can either keep the same rhythm or initiate a new one. Beyond review, this game is great for developing memory, listening, and music skills.

 Line or Circle Dancing

Everyone loves the Bunny Hop! Play some music with a definite beat. Then lead a line dance or circle dance or square dance. If you really get into it, you can substitute lyrics that relate to current lessons. Parent volunteers with some dance experience can really help make it fun and educational for everyone.

Creative Handshakes

Simple, quick, and fun! With music playing in the background, have learners introduce themselves to three or four other students by developing a unique personal handshake with each of them.

Cross-Laterals

Great state changer! With music in the background, have the group stand and follow the leader's cross-lateral motions. Touch hands to opposite knees; touch opposite elbows; touch opposite shoulders; give yourself a pat on the back to opposite side; touch opposite heels; touch nose with one hand and hold opposite ear with other hand while switching quickly; do "lazy 8s" in front of you by tracing the pattern of the number eight with thumb-up sign (start the 8 at the center, arms length, going up and to the right, do big loops on both sides and switch sides); do air swimming—one arm circles forward while the other circles backwards.

Follow the Leader

Great skills practice! The leader walks around the inside of the room and asks everyone to follow. As the leader states a word, the followers state words that rhyme. A variation on this game is to have the leader state a vocabulary word the class has learned and to have the group follow with the definition; or the leader states a multiplication equation and the group answers it.

Introduction Charades

A great challenge! Stand and find a partner. Tell that partner three things about yourself without speaking; use only charades. Then reverse roles. Afterwards, confirm what your partner was trying to tell you. A variation on this is to demonstrate three things about your school, your company, an idea, etc.

High Five's

We all need validation now and again! With music in the background, have everyone stand and find a partner. Following the leader's example, give your partner a high five, a low five, a high ten, a low ten, a high three, a low seven, a behind-the-back slap, etc. Then ask for volunteers to teach other creative and unique slaps.

Stretch and Breathe

Catch your breath! With relaxing background music playing, everyone follows the leader's stretching and breathing prompts. Encourage slow stretching movements, not bouncing. A variation is to lead learners in Tai Chi movements or dance steps.

Team Massage

A perfect way to downshift or close a session! With relaxing music playing in the background, ask everyone to stand up and form a circle. Then ask them to put their left shoulder towards the center so that everyone is facing the same direction. Then have them raise their hands above their heads and lower them on to the shoulders of the player in front of them. Now each person gives and receives a shoulder massage.

Opposites Attract

Great thinking exercise! With a partner, one student picks out an object in the room and the other then looks for something that is similar in some way or opposite; then the first person continues the exercise, looking for something either like or unlike the present object, and the game continues until the time is up. A more difficult variation on this game is to do it silently.

Passing Fun

A great way to start the day! With music playing in the background, have the group form a large circle or break into smaller groups of five or six students. Each member introduces him or herself by saying his/her name in conjunction with a funny facial expression. The group imitates the expression. A variation is to go around the circle one by one and repeat the facial expression and name of each person before them. Another variation is to have one player start a facial expression and pass it on to the player next to them who proceeds in the same manner (i.e., like the telephone game). Once the expression has been passed all the way around the circle, a new player starts the cycle again. Another more challenging variation is to pass a facial expression in one direction and a sound in the other.

Read My Mind

Good for a wild break! Display three "crazy faces" (facial expressions) and have the group practice them for a few minutes. Then have learners pair up and stand back-to-back while each silently picks one of the three faces. On cue, they turn around and see if their faces match. This is a variation on the old rock-paper-scissor game.

18 Psychic Handshake

Give yourself a hand! Ask everyone to stand and think of a number between one and three. Then have them introduce themselves to others with a corresponding handshake. If their number is two, they shake twice. If the handshakes match, you have succeeded in using your psychic powers, and you both raise your hands and say, "Winner!" If, however, your handshake is mismatched, you raise your hands and say, "Learning!" Game proceeds until everyone (or nearly everyone) has matched handshakes. Then everyone gets a hand.

19 Simon Says

An old-fashion favorite! Have everyone stand and follow "Simon," as you give a host of commands. When you don't preface the command with "Simon says...." and the learners follow anyway, they get to start over. Rather than disqualifying players, make it a win-win for everyone. Have the game end after five or ten minutes, rather than when no players remain in the game. There are many variations on this old theme: You can emphasize (1) listening skills; (2) name learning (Simon says, point to Darlene.); (3) geography/compass points (Simon says, point in the direction of Alaska.); (4) math skills (Simon says, use your body to provide the answer to 5 plus 3=...); (5) foreign language skills (Simon says, point to su boca or su mano.); (6) science concepts (Simon says, point to something in this room made of steel, glass, plastic, or a material that would not have existed fifty years ago.); and (7) anatomy (Simon says, point to your tibia bone.).

20 Arm's Length

Everybody can play! Have learners pair up and together measure three things in the room using a body part (i.e., fingers, hands, arms, foot, etc.). At the end of five minutes, the pairs report their results to the group. For example, "this cabinet is 210 knuckles long."

21 Roller Derby

With music playing in the background, have students stand up and walk fast around the entire room like a roller derby to increase circulation. Ask them to think of two to five key words discussed in the last twenty minutes. Then have them share their words with five other people. Set a few rules first to ensure safety, time limitations, courtesy, noise level, etc.

Relaxing Reviews

Great pretest review method! With calming music playing in the background, have learners get comfortable and close their eyes. After a few deep breaths, provide a concise review of the learning material. For example, "We learned today that the Mayan civilization flourished in Central America and Mexico between AD 250 and 900." Have learners raise their hand if they wish to contribute a learning review of their own.

A Change in Perspective

Make a fresh start! To keep the room novel and the learners' perspective fresh, have everyone stand up and find a seat on the opposite side of the room. A variation on this is to have everyone push their desks or chairs into a new position (i.e., a large circle, theater style, etc.).

Touch and Go

Exercise body and brain! Provide groups of four or five learners each with a scavenger assignment. For example, "go find and touch in sequence five things that are gold, four things that are silver, three glass items, two rubber items, and one plastic item." Variations on this can include content reviews. For example, "touch five right angles, four cylinders, three cubes, two rectangles, and one cone." Or have learners follow your commands in a foreign language. For example, "cinco verde, quatro azul, tres blanco, dos negro, y uno rojo."

Aesop's Fables

Bring out the actor in learners! Form teams. Then have each group identify the key concepts from the day's/week's lesson and incorporate them into a performance piece which follows a familiar theme from a childhood fable (i.e., Little Red Riding Hood, The Three Little Pigs, Cinderella, etc.). Ask teams to write out the story in seven to ten sentences first beginning with "Once upon a time..." and ending with "And they all lived happily ever after." Each team then performs their adapted fable for the enjoyment of the whole group.

What's In a Name?

Great brain break! Everyone stands up and writes their first name with their elbow, their middle name with their other elbow, their last name with their foot, and their mom or dad's name with their head.

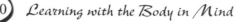

Add-Ons

A fun way to review! Invite one person to come up to the front of the room and act out something they've learned in class; then they freeze and another person is selected to come up and continue the impromptu learning charade; then one at a time, others join, adding on until one giant human scenario has taken place which ultimately represents the current lesson.

Bingo

Add enjoyment and learning value! Played in the traditional manner or with a creative variation that encourages more physical movement, bingo can make any review process more fun. Rather than supplying an answer as in traditional bingo, the leader asks a question. The players must then determine the answer before they can mark it on their bingo card. A more kinesthetic bingo can be played by outlining the floor with nine boxes, each with an answer taped to it. To mark an answer, the team sends a player to stand in the corresponding box. This approach can make for a friendly team competition.

Children's Song Re-make

Singing is good for the soul! Form teams. Then have each group identify the key concepts from the day's/week's lesson and incorporate them into a performance piece that can be sung to the tune of a familiar childhood song (i.e., Twinkle, Twinkle Little Star, She'll Be Coming 'Round the Mountain, Row, Row, Row the Boat, etc.) Ask teams to write out their lyrics and then sing their adapted song for the rest of the class.

Circle "Run-Ons"

Another good review technique! Write a review topic and related unfinished sentence up on the board. For example, "Topic: Movement Activities; Opening sentence: Energizers are best for..." Ask students, who are organized into small groups, to complete the sentence and add an unfinished one before turning it over to the next person in the group to do the same. The goal is to continue contributing to the review as long as possible.

Commercial Breaks

Give them a break! Divide the group into teams and give them time to prepare a commercial break related to the current unit of study or content. At various times throughout the day or week, ask a team to present their commercial break to the rest of the class.

Dueling Puppets

A novel review method! Using sock puppets or store-bought puppets (the kind with a moving mouth), create characters that represent the leader/teacher (on one hand) and a student (on the other hand). Perform a dialogue with the puppets that represents or reviews the current topic of learning.

Expert Interviews

A great one-on-one review technique! Divide the group in half with one group representing "the experts" and the other half representing "the reporters." The reporters job is to interview the experts on the present topic of study. Give them five minutes to "get the story," then reverse the roles so that the experts are now the reporters.

Game Shows

Games make learning fun! Using one of the popular TV game shows as a model (i.e., Jeopardy, Wheel of Fortune, Hollywood Squares, Who Wants to Be a Millionaire?, etc.), create a set of questions that relate to your present topic of learning. Incorporate the questions into the game show of your choice.

I Did It My Way

Get up and boogie! Divide the group into smaller groups of four or five learners each. Ask teams to identify ten key words or concepts from the present topic of learning. Then have the teams develop a song and dance routine that incorporates these topics.

Role Reversals

Take a walk on the wild side! Ask learners to find a partner. Then give them a period of time to prepare a lesson to give to the class on the present topic of study. Adjust the criteria of the assignment to fit the particular group needs (age, experience level, learning goals, etc.).

Line-Ups

Great comparing and contrasting practice! Ask the class to line up based on a specific criteria. It might be height, for instance, from tallest to shortest or birthdays from oldest to youngest. A variation on this game is called "Either Or." The leader stands in the middle of the room and says, "Move to the left side of the room if you're more like an apple and to the right if you're more like a pineapple." Of course the comparisons can be more challenging and values oriented such as, "Move to the left side of the room if you believe in corporal punishment and to the right if you don't." Make a list beforehand so you can keep the exercise moving quickly.

Math Magic

Number fun! Ask learners to find a partner, face each other, and put their hands behind their back. Then ask them to identify a number from zero to ten displayed by their fingers hidden behind their back. On your cue, they turn around quickly and show their number. The first partner to shout out the total of both numbers wins. Variations on the game can challenge learners' other math skills, as well, such as subtraction or multiplication equations.

Musical Chairs

An old standby that everyone loves! Have the group form a circle with chairs facing inward. The leader manages the music, while the group circles around the chairs. When the music stops, everyone must find a chair, but one has been removed. The person left standing must share one thing they've learned related to the present topic of study. Instead of disqualifying this player, however, continue the game until a variety of people have shared what they know.

My Friend

Great get-to-know-ya game! Ask everyone to find a partner. Set a time limit and ask one partner to interview the other. After a preestablished period of time, the roles are reversed. Afterwards, individuals introduce their partner to the rest of the class. This activity builds language, thinking, speaking, and memory skills.

Know Your Neighbor 41

Break the ice!

a. Introduce yourself to as many others as you can until the music stops.

b. Find three others with the same birthday month as you.

c. Get the names of three people taller than you, three shorter than you, and one person your same height.

d. Share with your partner where, when, and how you first learned the song being played (play childhood songs, anthems, etc.).

e. Stand up if you're right handed. Stand up if you're wearing blue. Stand up if you have brown eyes, etc.

f. Form a circle of chairs with a leader in the middle. The leader says, "All my neighbors who like panda bears, find a new seat." Or, "All my neighbors who have ever gone camping, find a new seat."

Pair-Share 42

Shop talk! Have everyone choose a partner. Write out the assignment on the board or post it. It might be something like the following: (1) Talk about a learning challenge you've experienced; (2) Discuss a concept you're not quite sure you understand; (3) Share one thing you found interesting about the present topic of study; and (4) Translate the key concepts learned today into the vocabulary of a two-, five-, or ten-year-old.

Poster Potpourri 43

Have everyone walk around the room and view the posters or artwork you have displayed. After five minutes or so, ask learners to locate a partner and share with that person your three favorite posters/pieces. You can post some questions on the board such as, What attracts you to this particular piece? How is this poster meaningful to you? In what way do you identify with this artwork?

Retro Visit 44

A little bit of history! Ask the group to stand, close their eyes, and imagine the world twenty, fifty, or one-hundred years earlier. Now prompt their imagination with such questions as the following: How would you talk? What topics would you find yourself discussing with others? What objects are in the room? What objects do we have today that would be missing during that era?

Spatial Memory

Move in the right direction! Teach a locational system (i.e., compass points, orienteering, map reading, etc.) by representing key points or concepts with particular words, colors, room locations, sounds, and/or feelings.

Team Affirmations

Lookin' good! In small groups, players stand and read aloud a list of team-building, psych-up affirmations that you have previously printed and distributed to each team member. The team leader goes first, then, while still standing, they rotate around quickly.

All the World's a Stage

Act and learn! Form small groups of three to five learners each. The team assignment is to develop a one- to three-minute act or role-play that reflects the present topic of learning. For example, if your present unit of study is the solar system, the group might act out the motions, size, or distance of the planets complete with the sun, moon, astro debris, and comets.

Toddler Talk

Simplify, simplify, simplify! In small groups, have learners translate the present topic of study into a lesson that five-year-olds would be able to understand. Provide a selection of props and visual aids for teams to work with. This is a great strategy to ensure everyone understands the basic concepts.

What's My Line

Get organized! The leader poses a question such as, what is your favorite midnight snack? Or, what brand of car do you drive? Or, what is your favorite color? Or, what farm animal are you most like? The large group divides into smaller groups based on similar answers.

Don't Look at Me

Keep 'um lookin'! Have the group form a circle. Ask everyone to look downward towards the middle of the circle. When the leader says "look up!" everyone looks up and into the eyes of another person in the circle. If two players match eyes, they step out of the circle. The last person in the circle is the "winner."

String Squares

What a square! Form teams of approximately four learners each and provide them with a ten-foot length of thick string or rope. The goal is to form a square with the string using team members as corners or posts. The challenge, however, is that they have to do it blindfolded, without talking, or without touching each other. You would be surprised how much strategizing and teamwork this simple nonverbal communication exercise requires.

In-Sync Counting

Out for the count! In groups of ten, ask learners to count simultaneously from one to ten and to begin on the leader's cue. The challenge is that the group cannot discuss strategy, and if two players say a number simultaneously, the group must start over. Everyone must participate and no one can talk, other than to claim a number.

Best Outdoor Games

Ball Toss

Catch the spirit! Form a circle of five to seven learners each a few feet apart. Give each group a ball, Frisbee, or bean bag. One person begins the toss, and the person who catches the object must share something they've learned during the day or week. Then they toss the object to another person who then shares something they've learned. A variation on this is to set a criteria like state capitals, song titles, math facts, world religions, etc. Play some music in the background and keep the game moving quickly.

Gordian Knot

All tied up! Have groups of six to eight learners each stand in a circle facing inward about two feet apart. Reaching across the circle with the right hand first and then the left, players clasp a hand opposite theirs. The challenge is to get out of the human knot without releasing hands. Success is possible.

Lap Sit

Loafin' again! Have the group stand in a large circle facing the back of the person in front of them and about six inches apart. When the leader gives the "sit" cue, everyone holds on to the waist of the person in front of them and gently sits down on the lap of the person behind them. Perfect timing spells success. This activity offers a great lesson in teamwork.

Military March

Hi-ho and away we go! Like the rhythmic chants military recruits use, the whole group practices a basic chorus: "It's really easy; see-say-do; if we can learn it; so can you." Then the group is divided up into teams and asked to create a follow-up verse that reflects a key concept from the present unit of study. For example, "Memory is a piece of cake; mnemonic tricks can help you rate; rhyming verse and peg-words too; one-two buckle my shoe." To conclude the exercise, one team at a time sings their made-up verse followed up by the whole group's rendition of the chorus.

Hopscotch

Old fashioned fun while reviewing! Lay out a hopscotch course on the floor (inside or outside) with chalk or string. On each square, put a number which corresponds to a question written up on the board or on poster board. If the player cannot answer the question, they go back to the line and await their next turn. If they are able to answer it, however, they get to keep going.

Walking Reviews

Out of their chairs and into fresh air! Provide learners with a list of review questions or give them the time to write up their own. Have learners choose a partner and go for a ten-minute walk together to review their lists of questions. Be sure to define an area and boundaries depending on their age (i.e., the playground for elementary students) that is suitable for the activity).

Jump-Rope Ditties

Get them hoppin'! Ask learners to make a list of the key concepts and words from the current unit of study. Then organize them into groups of three each and ask them to create a jump-rope ditty that incorporates their main concepts. Once their ditty is done, they get to go outside and practice it while honing their jump-rope skills simultaneously. Rotate roles so that everyone gets to jump and turn the rope.

Triple Tag

Triple fun! A giant game of tag in which everybody is "it." Participants run around tagging other players. Once you've been tagged, you must hold that part of your body with one hand, but you're still in the game. The second time you're tagged, you must hold that part of your body with the other hand. The third time you're tagged, you're frozen in place. The last one still going wins the game. Footnote: The same person cannot tag you more than once.

Tug of War

Let's get physical! Remember Tug-of-War? Well how about a variation on this old theme called "Verbal Tug"? Have learners choose a partner and a debate topic from your list of possibilities. One partner argues one side of the debate while the other argues the other. The goal, of course, is to convince their partner in one minute or less why they are right or why their topic is more important. After the verbal debate, the whole class can release pent up energy with a giant Tug-of-War game with partners on opposite sides.

Giant Tic-Tac-Toe

Chalk out Tic-Tac-Toe boxes on the blacktop or patio. Divide group into teams of five players each. Designate teams as either Xs or Os with a sheet of paper taped to their shirt. One teacher or helper is needed for each Tic-Tac-Toe game to facilitate the question asking. Each team, in turn, is asked a question that relates to the current unit of study. If the team answers correctly, they send a player to cover a box of their choice and questioning continues. If the team provides an incorrect answer, play alternates to the other team. The object of the game, of course, is to complete a line of Xs or Os.

Measuring Up

Make it real; make it meaningful! Provide each team of two to four learners each with a ruler, measuring tape, length of string, and a map of a nearby area depicting items such as a jungle gym, fence, sandbox, drinking fountain, and lunch tables. Beside each item, leave a space to write in the specific measurement (i.e., How many feet is the jungle gym from top to bottom?). The mission is to complete all measurements within a certain time frame. When the teams return for a debriefing, facilitate a discussion on time-saving techniques (i.e., Measuring the height of one box on the jungle gym and then multiplying that number by the number of boxes the jungle gym is high).

Trust Walk

Who do you trust? After a thorough discussion around the concepts of trust, responsibility, and consequences, have learners pair up. Give each team a blindfold and instruct them decide who will be the leader and who will be the follower. Ultimately, learners will play both roles. Provide a time limit (i.e., five minutes) and instruct leaders to guide their partners on a walk where they describe for the blindfolded partner where they are and what surrounds them. Ring a bell when it's time to switch roles. Hold a debriefing session after the walks where learners discuss what it felt like to play each role.

Obstacle Course

Ready for a physical and mental workout? Map out an obstacle course (preferably a large loop) with a few learners stationed at "question points" along the way and a few timers at the start/finish line. Lead all learners through a practice session stopping at each "question point" for a sample review question while proceeding through the physical obstacles, as well. Once everyone is comfortable with the course, start players on the course, one at a time, spaced about thirty seconds apart. The object is for learners to beat their own previous times. Questioners provide one question after another until the player answers one correctly. Rotate roles so that everyone has a few chances to run the obstacle course and act as a questioner.

Brainy Energizers
Allow 30-90 Seconds for Each

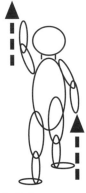

Apple Picking

Fast pace; quick breathing.
Stand in place; reach for the sky.
Alternate with left hand and right
leg up; then right hand and left leg up.

Run and Touch Scavenger Hunts

Fast pace. Find and touch 5 objects
(colors, locations, etc.) in 1 minute.
Create variations on the theme.

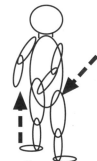

Cross-Laterals

Moderate pace; slow, deep breathing.
Stand in place, touch opposite elbows,
then shoulders, knees, ankles, and hips.
Create variations.

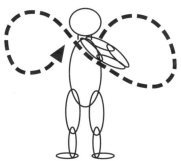

Barn-Storming

Stand in place; slow deep breathing.
Clasp hands in front of you (like
make-believe airplane wings); now soar
left and right, high and low, as you make
horizontal figure eights.

Focusing the Brain

Do One of These for 30-90 Seconds

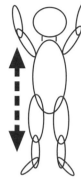

Sky Stretchers

Stand in place; slow, deep breathing. Slowly stretch upwards. First raise arms, then extend and stretch up onto your toes. Hold for 5 seconds, then release.

Mind Calmers

Sit with legs crossed and hands clasped. Inhale slowly as if receiving the gift of life. Exhale slowly with deep gratitude.

Circulation Boosters

Sit with legs stretched out in a relaxing position. Using both hands, gently massage eyes, ears, and forehead. Inhale and exhale with slow deep breaths.

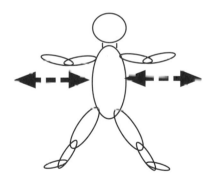

Mind Openers

Stand in place with legs spread as wide as possible; take slow, deep breaths. Slowly stretch arms and palms outwards; arch back, extend and hold for 5 seconds, then release.

APPENDIX

Bibliography

Allen, G.; R. Buxton; E. Wong; and E. Courchesne. 1997. Attentional activation of the cerebellum independent of motor movement. *Science*. March 28; 5308: 1940-43.

Allman, J. M. 1999. *Evolving brains*. New York, NY: Scientific American Library.

Allman, W. 1992. The mental edge. *U.S. News & World Report*. August 3; (52).

Anderson, Ian. 1991. What is making these people sick? *Chemecology*. February; (2): 2-3.

Ayers, Jean. 1991. *Sensory integration and learning disorders*. Los Angeles, CA: Western Psychological Services.

———1972. *Sensory integration and the child*. Los Angeles, CA: Western Psychological Services.

Bandura, A. 1977. *Social learning theory*. Englewood Cliffs, NJ: Prentice-Hall.

Barker, R.; and S. Barasi. 1999. *Neuroscience at a glance*. Oxford, London: Blackwell Science, Ltd.

Bent, Kathy. 1999. The PASS model is a model for total school reform. <kbent@amersports.org.

Benton, D.; and G. Roberts. 1988. Effect of vitamin and mineral supplementation of intelligence of a sample of school children. *Lancet*. Jan 23; 1(8578): 140-3.

Benton, W. (ed.) 1986. "Montessori System" in Encyclopedia Britannica. Chicago, IL. Vol. 17.

Beyers, John. 1998. The biology of play. *Child Development*. June; 69 (3): 599-600.

Biering-Sorensen, F. 1984. A one-year perspective study of low back trouble in a general population. *Danish Medical Bulletin*. Oct. 32 (5): 373.

Bjorklund, D. F.; and R. D. Brown. 1998. Physical play and cognitive development: Integrating activity, cognition, and education. *Child Development*. June; 69 (3): 604-06.

Black, J. E.; K. R. Issacs; B. J. Anderson; A. A. Alcantara; and W. T. Greenough. 1990. Learning causes synaptogenesis while motor activity causes angiogenesis in cerebellar cortex of adult rats. Proceedings of the National Academy of Sciences. 87: 5568-72.

Boulton, M.; and P. K. Smith. 1992. The social nature of play fighting and play chasing: Mechanisms and strategies underlying cooperation and compromise. In J. H. Barkow, L. Cosmides and J.Tooby (eds.) *The adapted mind: Evolutionary psychology and the generation of culture*. New York/Oxford: Oxford University Press.

Boone, R. T.; and J. G. Cunningham. 1998. Children's decoding of emotion in expressive body movement; the development of cue attunement. *Developmental Psychology*, Sept.; 34(5):1007-16.

Bredekamp, S.; and C. Copple. 1997. Developmentally appropriate practice in early childhood programs. (Rev. ed.) Wash. D.C. National Association for the Education of Young Children Booklet.

Bushnell, Emily; and Paul Boudreau. 1993. Motor development and the mind: The potential role of motor abilities as a determinant of aspects of perceptual development. *Child Development*. 64 (4): 1005-21.

Byers, J. A.; and C. Walker. 1995. Refining the motor training hypothesis for the evolution of play. *American Naturalist*. (146): 25-40.

Cahill, L.; B. Prins; M. Weber; and J. McGaugh. 1994. Adrenergic activation and memory for emotional events. *Nature*. Oct. 20; 371 (6499): 702-4.

Calvin, William. 1996. *How brains think*. New York, NY: Basic Books/ Harper Collins.

Cammisa, K. 1994. Educational kinesiology with learning disabled students. *Perceptual and Motor Skills*. 78: 105-06.

Carmichael, K.; and D. Atchinson. 1997. Music and play therapy: Playing my feelings. *International Journal of Play Therapy*. 6: 63-72.

Chase, M. 1999. New behavior therapy for kids uses touch, tones, and trampolines. *Wall Street Journal*, Oct. 29; pg. B1.

Clair, Robin. 1996. The effects of tactile stimulation and gross motor movement on cognitive learning: A test of Montessori's muscular movement theory in the classroom. ERIC file #ED334611.

Cranz, G. 1998. *The chair: Rethinking culture, body and design*. New York, NY: W. W. Norton & Co.

Curry, N. 1977. Considerations of current basic issues on play. In N. Curry (Ed.) *Play: The child strives for self-realization*. Washington, D.C.: Booklet for National Association of the Education of Young Children.

Dennison, Paul; and Gail Dennison. 1989. *Brain Gym: Teacher's Edition*. Ventura, CA: Edu-Kinesthetics, Inc.

Dhyan, Sutorius. 1995. The transforming force of laughter with the focus on the laughing meditation. *Patient Education and Counseling*. Sept. 26 (1-3): 367-371.

Dienstbier, Richard. 1989. Arousal of physiological toughness: Implications for mental and physical health. *Psychological Review*. Vol 96(1), Jan 1989, 84-100.

Dixon, W.; and C. Shore. 1997. Tempermental predictors of linguistic style during multiword acquisition. *Infant Behavior & Development*. Jan-March; 20(1) 99-103.

Dwyer, Terence; Leigh Blizzard; and Kimberlie Dean. 1996. Physical activity and performance in children. *Nutrition Reviews*. April; 54(4): 27-32.

Easterbrook, J. A. 1959. The effects of emotion on cue utilization and the organization of behavior. *Psychological Review*. 66: 183-201.

Eastman, M.; and E. Kamon. 1976. Posture and subjective evaluation at flat and slanted desks. *Human Factors*. Feb; 18(1): 15-26.

Edelman, M. (ed.) 1995. Did you know that having fun may be good for your health. Jan. 1; *Bottom Line Personal*. p. 7.

Elders, J. 1994. May 13; U. S. Surgeon General's speech to Woman's Sport Foundation.

Ericksson, P. S.; E. Perfilieva; T. Bjork-Eriksson; A. M. Alborn; C. Nordborg; D. A. Peterson; and F. Gage. 1998. Neurogenesis in the adult human hippocampus. *Nature Medicine*. Nov; 4(11): 1313-17.

Fery, Y. A.; A. Fery; A. Hofe, A.Vom; and M. Rieu. 1997. Effects of physical exhaustion on cognitive functioning. *Perceptual and Motor Skills*. 84: 291-297.

Fordyce, D. E.; J. M. Wehner. 1993. Physical activity enhances spatial learning performance with an associated alteration in hippocampal protein kinase C activity in C57BL/6 and DBA/2 mice. *Brain Research*. Aug; 619(1-2): 111-19.

Frost, J. L. 1996. *Play and playscapes*. Albany, NY: Delmar Publishing.

Gabbard, C. 1998. Windows of opportunity for early brain and motor development. *Journal of Physical Education, Recreation, and Dance*. 69(54-55): 61.

Gabbard, C.; and J. Barton. 1979. Effects of physical activity on mathematical computation among young children. *Journal of Psychology*. 103: 287-8.

Gao, J.; L. M. Parsons; J. Bower; J. Xiong; and P. Fox. 1996. Cerebellum implicated in sensory acquisition and discrimination rather than motor control. *Science*. April 26; 5261: 545-7.

Gardner, H. 1999. *The disciplined mind*. New York, NY: Simon & Schuster.

Gerber, Susan. 1996. Extracurricular activities and academic achievement. *Journal of Research and Development in Education*. 30(1): 42-50.

Gershon, M. 1998. *The second brain*. New York, NY: Harper-Collins.

Gibbons, D.; V. Ebbeck; and M. Weiss. 1995. Fair play for kids: Effects on the moral development of children in physical education. *Quarterly for Exercise and Sport*. Sept; 66(3): 247.

Gilbert, A. G. 1977. *Teaching the three Rs through movement experiences*. New York: Macmillan Publishing.

Gillberg, M.; I. Anderzen; T. Akerstedt; and K. Sigurdson. 1986. Urinary catecholamine responses to basic types of physical activity. *European Journal of Applied Physiology*. 55: 575-78.

Goleman, D. 1995. *Emotional intelligence*. New York, NY: Bantam Books.

Gomez-Pinilla, F.; L. Dao; and V. So. 1997. Physical exercise induces FGF-2 and its mRNA in the hippocampus. *Brain Research*. August 1; 764(1-2): 1-8.

Greenwald, A. G. 1992. New look: Unconscious cognition reclaimed. *American Psychologist*. 47: 766-79.

Gregory, Lynn. 1995. The "turnaround" process: Factors influencing the school success of urban youth. *Journal of Adolescent Research*. Jan; 10(1): 136-54.

Greico, A. 1986. Sitting posture: An old problem and a new one. *Ergonomics*. 29(3): 345-62.

Griffing, P. 1980. The relationship between socioeconomic status and sociodramatic play among black kindegarten children. Genetic Psychology Monographs. 101: 3-34.

Grimsrud, T. 1990. Humans were not created to sit-and why you have to refurnish your life. *Ergonomics*. 33(3): 291.

Gunnar, M. R. 1996. Quality of care and the buffering of stress psychology: Its potential in protecting the developing human brain. Minneapolis, MN. University of Minnesota Institute of Child Development Program.

Hallet, M. 1999. Gray matters: sports, fitness and the brain. Transcript from National Public Radio. Dr. Mark Hallet was interviewed by Frank Gifford. May 1999. Available @ (800) 652-7246.

Hamann, D.; R. Bourassa; and M. Aderman. 1991. Arts experiences and creativity scores of high school students. *Contributions of Music Education*. 14: 36-7.

Hanna, J. L. 1995. The power of dance. *Journal of Alternative Complementary Medicine*. Winter; 1(4): 323-31.

———1979. Dance and social structure: The Ubakla of Nigeria. *Journal of Communication*. 29(4): 184-91.

Hanna, T. 1993. The Body of life: Creating new pathways for sensory awareness and fluid movement. Rochester, VT: Healing Arts Press.

Hannaford, Carla. 1995. *Smart Moves*. Arlington, VA: Great Ocean Publishing.

Harmon, D. B. 1951. The coordinated classroom. Research paper: The American Seating Company, Grand Rapids, MI.

Henning, Robert; P. Jacques; G. Kissel; and A. Sullivan. 1997. Frequent short breaks from computer work: Effects on productivity and well-being at two field sites. *Ergonomics*. Jan; 40(1): 78-91.

Hettinger, T. 1985. Occupational hazards associated with diseases of the skeletal system. *Ergonomics*. 28(1): 69-75.

Hotz, R. 1999. Active mind, body linked to brain growth. *Los Angeles Times*. Feb. 23;. pg. A1.

Huse, D. 1995. Restructuring the physical context: Redesigning learning environments. *Children's Environments*. 12(3): 290-310.

Iacoboni, Marco; Roger Woods; Marcel Brass; Harold Bekkering; John Mazziotta; and Giacomo Rizzolatti. 1999. Cortical mechanisms of human imitation.. Dec.24; 286: 2526-28.

Jeannerod, Marc. 1997. *The cognitive neuroscience of action*. Cambridge, MA: Blackwell Publishers.

Jennings, P. J.; and S. W. Keele. 1991. *A computational model of attentional requirements in sequence learning*. Proceedings of the 13th annual conference of the Cognitive Science Society. Hillsdale, NJ: Earlbaum Publishing.

Jensen, Eric. 1998. *Teaching with the brain in mind*. Alexander, VA: Association for Curriculum and Development.

Johnston, V. 1999. *Why we feel: The science of human emotions*. Las Cruces, NM: New Mexico State University.

Karr-Morse, Robin; and Meredith Wiley. 1997. *Ghosts From the Nursery*. New York: The Atlantic Monthly Press.

Kavale, K.; and P. D. Mattson. 1983. One jumped off the balance beam: Meta-analysis of perceptual motor training. *Journal of Learning Disabilities*. 16: 165-73.

Kay, S.; and R. Subotnik. 1994. Talent beyond words: Unveiling spatial, expressive, kinesthetic, and musical talent in young children. *Gifted Child Quarterly*. 38: 70-4.

Kearney, P. 1996. Brain research shows importance of arts in education. *The Star Tribune*. August 3;. p. 19A.

Kempermann, G; and F. Gage. 1999. New nerve cells for the human brain. *Scientific American*. May; 208(5): 48-53.

Kempermann, G.; H. Kuhn; and F. Gage. 1998. Experience-induced neurogenesis in senescent dentate gyrus. *Journal of Neuroscience*. May 1; 18(9): 3206-12.

Kermoian, R.; and J. J. Campos. 1988. Locomotor experience: A facilitator of spatial cognitive development. *Child Development*. Aug; 59(4): 908-17.

Kesslak, J., V. Patrick; J. So; C. Cotman; and F. Gomez-Pinilla. 1998. Learning upregulates brain-derived neurotrophic factor messenger ribonucleic acid: A mechanism to facilitate encoding and circuit maintenance. *Behavioral Neuroscience*. Aug; 112(4): 1012-19.

Khalsa, G. C. 1988. Effect of educational kinesiology on static balance of learning disabled students. *Perceptual and Motor Skills*. 67: 51-54.

Kramer, A. 1999. Aging, fitness and neurocognitive function. *Nature*. July 29; 400: 418-19.

Kratus, J. 1994. Relationships among children's audiation and their compositional processes and products. *Journal of Research in Music Education*. 42: 115-130.

————1989. A Time analysis of the compositional processes used by children ages 7 to 11. *Journal of Research in Music Education*. 37: 5-20.

Krauss, Robert. 1998. Why do we gesture when we speak? *Current Directions in Psychological Science*. April; 7(2): 54-60.

Leroux, C.; and R. Grossman. 1999. Arts in the schools paint masterpiece: Higher scores. *Chicago Tribune*. Oct. 21; pg. A-1.

Levy, J. 1978. *Play behavior*. New York, NY: Wiley & Sons.

Liberman, J. 1991. *Light: Medicine of the future*. Santa Fe, NM: Bear & Company Publishing.

MacLaughlin, J.A.; R.R. Anderson; and M.F. Holic. 1982. Spectral character of sunlight modulates photosynthesis of previtamin D3 and its photo-isomers in human skin. *Science*. May; 216(4549); 1001-3.

Mandal, A. 1982. The correct height of school furniture. *Human Factors*. June; 24(3): 257-69.

————1981. The seated man (Momo Sedens): The seated work position—theory and practice. *Applied Ergonomics*. March; 12(1): 19-26.

Manza, L.; and A. Reber. 1992. Inter- and Intra- modal transfer of an implicitly acquired rule system. Unpublished manuscript.

Manzo, K. K. 1997. Physical attraction. *Education Week*. 16: 27.

Markais, E. A.; F. H. Gage. 1999. Adult-generated neurons in the dentate gyrus send axonal projections to field CA3 and are surrounded by synaptic vesicles. *Journal of Comparative Neurology*. April 19; 406(4): 449-60.

Martens, F. 1982. Daily physical education. *Journal of Physical Education, Recreation, and Dance*. 53(3) 55-8.

McCaslin, N. 1996. Creative drama in the classroom and beyond (6th ed.) White Plains, NY: Longman Press.

McClelland, J. L.; B. L. McNaughton; and R. C. O'Reilly. 1995. Why are there complementary learning systems in the hippocampus and neocortex: Insights from the success and failures of connectionist models of learning and memory. *Psychological Review*. 102: 419-57.

McCune, L. 1998. The Immediate and Ultimate Functions of Physical Activity Play. *Child Development*. June; 69(3): 601-3.

McNaughten, Dennis; and Carl Gabbard. 1993. Physical exertion and immediate mental performance of sixth-grade children. *Perceptual and Motor Skills*. 77: 1155-59.

McNeal, Ralph. 1995. Extracurricular activities and high-school dropouts. *Sociology of Education*. Jan; 68: 62-81.

Michaud, Ellen; and Russell Wild. 1991. *Boost your brain power*. Emmaus, PA: Rodale Press.

Michon, J. A. 1977. Holes in the fabric of subjective time. *Acta Psychol*. 41: 191-203.

Mohanty, B.; and A. Hejmandi. 1992. Effects of intervention training on some cognitive abilities of preschool children. *Psychological Studies*. 37: 31-7.

Mosseri, Rami. 1998. Changing the culture of violence: A seven day admission to a secure unit provides a powerful norm in residential care. *Residential Treatment for Children & Youth*. 16(1): 1-9.

Neumeister, A.; R. Goessler; M. Lucht; T. Kapitany; C. Bamas; and S. Kasper. 1996. Bright light therapy stabilizes the antidepressant effect of partial sleep deprivation. *Biological Psychiatry*. 39(1): 16-21, 1996 Jan 1.

Norton, Yvonne. 1970. A concept: Structuro-functional development leading toward early cognito-perceptual behavior. *Americal Journal of Occupational Therapy*. 24: 34-43.

Nouri, Shawn; and John Beer. 1989. Relations of moderate physical exercise to scores on hostility, aggression, and trait-anxiety. *Perceptual Motor Skills*. 68: 1191-1194.

Palmer, Lyelle. 1980. Auditory discrimination development through vestibulo-cochlear stimulation. *Academic Therapy*. Sept; 16(1): 55-68.

Palmer, Lyelle and Eric Jensen. 1995. Bright brain: Learning readiness stimulators (Video Program). San Diego, CA: The Brain Store.

Parkin. A. J.; and S. Streete. 1988. Implicit and explicit memory in young and older adults. *British Journal of Psychology*. 79: 361-69.

Parsons. L.; and P. Fox. 1997. Sensory and cognitive functions. *International Review of Neurobiology*. 41: 255-71.

Payne, G. 1995. *Human motor development: A life-span approach*. Mountain View, CA: Mayfield Publishing Co.

Pearce, J. C. 1992. *Evolution's end: Claiming the potential of our intelligence*. New York, NY: Harper-Collins.

Pellegrini, A. 1984. The effects of exploration and play on young children's associative fluency: A review and extension of training studies. In T.D. Yawkey & A. Pelligrini (Eds.) *Child's Play: Developmental and Applied*. pgs. 237-253. Hillsdale, NJ: Erlbaum & Assoc.

Pellegrini, A. D.; P. D. Huberty; and I. Jones. 1995. The effects of recess timing on children's playground and classroom behaviors. *American Educational Research Journal*. 32: 845-64.

Pellegrini, A. D.; and P. K. Smith. 1998a. Physical activity play: Consensus and debate. *Child Development*. June; 69(3): 598-610.

Pellegrini, A. D.; and P. K. Smith. 1998b. Physical activity play: The nature and function of a neglected aspect of play. *Child Development*. June; 69(3): 577.

Pert, C. 1997. *Molecules of emotion*. New York, NY: Simon & Schuster.

Peterson, C.; S. Maier; and M. Seligman. 1993. *Learned helplessness*. New York, NY: Oxford University Press.

Piaget, Jean. 1952. *The origins of intelligence in children*. (M. Cook, Trans.). New York, NY: International Universities Press.

Pintrich, P. R.; and E. H. Schunk. 1996. *Motivation in education: Theory, research, and application*. Englewood Cliffs, NJ: Prentice-Hall.

Pollatschek, J. J.; and F. J. O'Hagen. 1989. An investigation of the Psycho-physical influences of a quality daily physical education program. *Health Education Research*. Sept; 4(3): 341-50.

Posner, Michael; and Marcus Raichle. 1994. *Images of mind*. New York, NY: Scientific American.

Reber, Arthur. 1993. *Implicit learning and tacit knowledge*. New York, NY: Oxford University Press.

Reber, A.; F. F. Walkenfield; and R. Hernstadt. 1991. Implicit and explicit learning: Individual differences and IQ. *Journal of Experimental Psychology: Learning, Memory, and Cognition*. 17: 888-96.

Reisbrod, L.; and S. Greenland. 1985. Factors associated with self-reported back-pain prevalence: A population-based study. *Journal of Chronic Diseases*. 38(8): 691-702.

Richardson, S. 1996. Tarzan's little brain. *Discover Magazine*. 17(11): 100-2.

Rittel, H.; and M. Webber. 1973. Dilemmas in a general theory of planning. *Policy Science*. 4: 155-69.

Rizzolatti, G.; L. Fadiga; L. Fogassi; and V. Gallese. 1997. Enhanced: The space around us. *Science*. July 11; 5323: 190-1.

Sallis, J.; T. McKenzie; B. Kolody; M. Lewis; S. Marshall; and P. Rosengard. 1999. Effects of health-related physical education on academic achievement: Project SPARK. *Research quarterly for Exercise and Sport*. June; 70(2): 127.

Seefelt, V.; and P. Vogel. 1986. The value of physical activity. Reston, VA: AAHPERD & NASPE. ED 289 866.

Shaw, G. 2000. *Keeping Mozart in mind*. San Diego, CA: Academic Press.

Shephard, R. 1996. Habitual physical activity and academic performance. *Nutrition Reviews*. 54(4): S32-S35.

Sifft, J. and G. Khalsa. 1991. Effect of educational kinesiology upon simple response times and choice response times. *Perceptual and Motor Skills*. 73: 1011-15.

Silliker, S.; and J. Quirk. 1997. The effect of extracurricular activity participation on the academic performance of male and female high school students. *The School Counselor*. March; 44: 288-93.

Silverman, I.; and M. Eals. 1992. Sex differences in spatial ability: Evolutionary theory and data. In J. H. Barkow; L. Cosmides; and J. Tooby (eds.) *The adapted mind: Evolutionary psychology and the generation of culture*. New York and Oxford: Oxford University Press.

Simons-Morton, B.; P. Eitel; and M. Small. 1999. School physical education: Secondary analyses of the school health policies and programs study. *Journal of School Health*. 30(5).

Sparrow, W. A.; and B. J. Wright. 1993. Effect of physical exercise on cognitive tasks. *Perceptual and Motor Skill*. 77: 675-79.

Sperry, R. 1968. Hemisphere disconnection and unity in conscious awareness. *American Psychologist* 23: 723-33.

Spitzer, M. 1999. *The mind within the net*. Cambridge, MA: MIT Press.

Stevenson, H. W.; and S. Y. Lee. 1990. Contexts of achievement. Monographs of the Society for Research in Child Development. 55 (1-2) Serial no. 221.

Tanaka, M. 1999. Emotional stress and characteristics of brain noradrenaline release in the rat. *Industrial Health*. April; 37(2): 143-56.

Templeton, Rosalyn; and Rita Jensen. 1996. Can adding movement to learning improve the classroom environment? Paper presented at the Annual meeting of the American Educational Research Association. (New York, NY, April 8-12, 1996) ERIC file locator #412199.

Terr, L. 1999. *Beyond love and work: Why adults need to play*. New York, NY: Scribner/Simon & Schuster.

Thayer, R. 1996. *The origin of everyday moods*. New York, NY: Oxford University Press.

Tizard, B.; and M. Hughes. 1976. *Young children learning*. Cambridge, MA: Harvard University Press.

Tomporowski, Phillip; and Norman Ellis. 1986. Effects of exercise on cognitive processes: A review. *Psychological Bulletin*. 99(3): 338-46.

van Hoorn, J.; T. Nourot; B. Scales; and K. Alward. 1993. *Play as the center of the curriculum*. New York, NY: Macmillan Books.

van Praag, H.; G. Kempermann; and F. Gage. 1999. Running increases cell proliferation in the adult mouse dentate gyrus. *Nature Neuroscience*. March; 2(3): 266-70.

Vygotsky, Lev. 1978. *Mind in society: The development of higher psychological processes* (M. Cole; V. John-Steiner; S. Scribner; and E. Souberman, Eds.). Cambridge: Harvard University Press.

Wagner, Matthew 1997. The effects of isotonic resistance exercise on aggression variable in adult male inmates in the Texas Department of Criminal Justice. Texas A & M University: UMI Order Number AAM9701731, Dissertation Abstracts International Section A: Humanities & Social Sciences: Feb., pg. 57 (8A): 3442.

Weiner, J.; and A. Brown. 1993. *Office biology*. New York, NY: MasterMedia Publications.

Wickelgren, Ingrid. 1999. Memory for order found in the motor cortex. *Science*. 283(5408): 1167.

Widmeyer, Neil; and Edward McGuire. 1997. Frequency of competition and aggression in professional ice hockey. *International Journal of Sport Psychology*. Jan-Mar 28; (1): 57-66.

Wilson, Frank. 1998. *The Hand*. New York, NY: Pantheon Books.

Wilson, M. A.; and B. L. McNaughton. 1994. Reactivation of hippocampal ensemble memories during sleep. *Science*. 265: 676-79.

Wohlwill, J. 1984. Relationships between play and exploration. In T. D. Yawkey; and A. D. Pellegrini (Eds.). *Child's play*. Hillsdale, NJ: Erlbaum Press.

Yamada, N.; M. Martin-Iverson; K. Daimon; T Tsujimoto; and S. Takahashi. 1995. Clinical and chronobiological effects of light therapy on non seasonal affective disorders. *Biological Psychiatry*. June 15; 37(12): 866-73.

Yan, J. H.; J. R. Thomas; and J. H. Downing. 1998. Locomotion improves children's spatial search: A meta-analytic review. *Perceptual Motor Skills*. August; 87(1): 67-82.

Young, Richard. 1964. Effect of prenatal drugs and neonatal stimulation on later behavior. *Journal of Comparative and Psyioligal Anatomy*. 58: 309-11.

Zacharkow, D. 1988. *Posture: Sitting, standing, chair design and exercise*. Springfield, IL. Charles Thomas Publishing. (Also see: "Sitting down on the job: Not as easy as it sounds." *Occupational Health and Safety*, 50(10) October 1981).

Brain-Based Resources

The Great Memory Book by Karen Markowitz & Eric Jensen
The Great Memory Book balances current research with practical tips for optimal memory fitness. From its primer on brain biology to in-depth discussions on neuronutrients and mnemonics, this book is a great tool for anyone wanting to achieve memory excellence.

Brain-Based Learning by Eric Jensen
A bonanza of neuroscience discovery is revealing astonishing insights about the brain and learning. These dramatic new models are a hybrid of powerful research on the role of emotions, bio-clocks, stress, threat, and environment. Hear what the Nobel laureates say about the brain, attention, thinking, and memory. The author then weaves the latest discoveries into something easy-to-implement the very next workday.

Smart Moves by Carla Hannaford
An excellent overview of the body-mind relationship. Easy to understand and written for educators at all levels. Best book on educational kinesiology.

Super Teaching by Eric Jensen
A Brain Store® best-seller!More than 1,000 practical strategies for energizers, openings, closings, environments, multiple intelligences, discipline practices, and brain research. Enough ideas for three years!

Bright-Brain Video Program by Lyelle Palmer & Eric Jensen
Learning readiness stimulators for children ages 4 to 8. Develop the proper neural patterning necessary for a bright brain. This video series builds a foundation for learning that will last a lifetime. You get two videos, a detailed instruction manual, and a full color poster.

Order any of the above resources from The Brain Store®. Unconditional satisfaction or money-back guarantee. Call (800) 325-4769 or fax (858) 546-7560. Free catalog included. Shop our website at: www.thebrainstore.com.

About the Author

A former teacher and current member of the International Society for Neuroscience, **Eric Jensen,** has taught at all education levels, from elementary through university. In 1981 Jensen co-founded SuperCamp, the nation's first and largest brain-compatible learning program for teens, which now claims more than 25,000 graduates. He is currently president of Jensen Learning, Corp., in San Diego, California. His other books include *Music with the Brain in Mind*, *Learning Smarter*, *Different Brains, Different Learners*, *The Great Memory Book*, *Teaching with the Brain in Mind*, *Brain-Compatible Strategies*, *Sizzle and Substance*, *Trainer's Bonanza*, and *Super Teaching*. He's listed in Who's Who Worldwide and remains deeply committed to making a positive, significant, and lasting difference in the way the world learns. Jensen is a sought-after conference speaker who consults and trains educators in the U.S. and abroad. **The author can be contacted at eric@jlcbrain.com.**

Index